The
Big DADGAD
Chord Book

An In-Depth Exploration
of DADGAD Guitar Tuning

HARVEY REID

WOODPECKER
MULTIMEDIA

York, Maine USA

ISBN: 978-1-63029-042-9

WOODPECKER
MULTIMEDIA

PO Box 815 York Maine 03909 USA

www.woodpecker.com

CONTENTS

History of DADGAD Tuning

Before 6-string guitars first appeared in Europe in between and 400 and 500 years ago, the various lutes, citterns, vihuelas and other fretted, plucked instruments were tuned in many different ways. From the scattered written information we have, we know that what is generally called "standard tuning" emerged victorious during the early 1800's, apparently evolving from the 5-course guitar that was commonly tuned ADGBE.

There is nothing "sacred" about standard tuning, and it is essentially a compromise of tuning the instrument in perfect 4ths, where each string is 5 frets from the next. All through the history of the guitar, players have commonly lowered the bass E string to D (usually called *Dropped D* or *Drop D* tuning), though with only one outer string changed, the result was always manageable, and a different experience than what we typically call an "altered tuning." A few guitarists like Carl Kress experimented with new tunings in the early 1900's, and in smaller niches like blues and Hawaiian guitar a number of non-standard tunings have always been commonly used, but for the most part as the guitar grew in popularity in jazz, country, classical and popular music in the 20th century and took its place as a mainstream instrument, it was always tuned E-A-D-G-B-E.

In the 1960's when a generation of musicians discovered American blues music, which relied heavily on non-standard tunings, it began a period of exploration of tunings by both instrumental guitarists and singer-songwriters. John Fahey was the pioneer, and he and Leo Kottke popularized open-tuning instrumental fingerpicking, spawning a sizable movement of what is often called "American primitive guitar." (Fahey first recorded in DADGAD tuning in 1964.) Guitarists would typically play in a number of tunings, and the idea that a serious guitarist would ignore standard tuning was just beginning. Small record labels like Tacoma Records, Windham Hill Records, and Kicking Mule Records featured almost entirely instrumental, open-tuned guitar, and players like Peter Lang, Robbie Basho, John Renbourn, Eric Schoenberg, Sandy Bull, Stefan Grossman, Will Ackerman and many others continued to spread the idea of non-standard tunings around, though it remained far from the mainstream. Instrumentalist Don Ross has used over 100 tunings in his body of work.

Songwriter Joni Mitchell has employed as many as 50 different tunings during her career, and popular singers in the 1970's like Crosby, Stills & Nash and Led Zeppelin created some of their best-known songs in new tunings. Keith Richards of the Rolling Stones began to play in Open G tuning exclusively in the 1970's, and the idea that new and musically exciting chords, resonances and voicings could be accessed by experimenting with the tuning, though still not widespread, was growing steadily, and most players at least knew there was such a thing as other tunings.

The story of DADGAD tuning begins with a group of British Isles acoustic guitarists, including John Renbourn, Bert Jansch, Martin Carthy and especially Davey Graham. The most common story is that Davey Graham came up with DADGAD tuning while visiting Morocco and being intrigued with its music and the skills of an oud player he encountered there. His 1962 version of *She Moved Through the Fair* is usually credited as being the first recorded piece in DADGAD tuning. The idea of using this new tuning to play traditional British Isles music spread very quickly, and players including Daithe Sproule, Mícheál Ó Domhnaill, Archie Fisher, John Faulkner, Paul Brady, Donal Lunny, Richard Thompson, Dick Gaughan, Michael Hedges, Nic Jones and many others began to create fresh new music and arrangements of traditional songs and tunes in DADGAD.

Moroccan-born French guitarist Pierre Bensusan took the tuning to a new level in the late 1970's and early 1980's when he released a series of stellar recordings. Bensusan inspired legions of followers, and became probably the first profoundly skilled solo guitarist to play exclusively in DADGAD tuning. Since that time, he has continued his crusade to create a large body of guitar music in this tuning, and to teach and spread it around as part of his life's work.

DADGAD tuning has remained popular in the Celtic guitar genre for decades, though in recent years it has continued to spread in popularity to other kinds of music. Pop songwriters, rock bands, and experimental guitarists have all discovered its charms, and it has now become one of the most commonly-used tunings, probably now in 2nd place behind Dropped-D.

Players of a number of styles are exploring it on a deeper level than most tunings, which makes a book like this useful. It is now common to find musicians who play only in DADGAD, or at least who keep an instrument always in this tuning.

Why Use DADGAD Tuning?

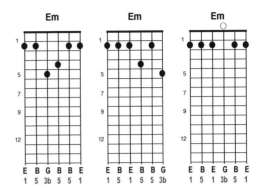

Em	Em	Em
E B G B B E	E B E B B G	E B E G B E
1 5 3b 5 5 1	1 5 1 5 5 3b	1 5 1 3b 5 1

If you have only used one tuning of the guitar, you may have trouble even understanding the advantages of using new tunings. Each time you retune the instrument, you have to start over learning the fingerboard, since the geometry of notes, chords and scales is different for each tuning. Anyone who has tried to play in a new tuning has experienced the confusion of not knowing where the music is, and losing all the familiar shapes and patterns. What takes longer to grasp is the concept and the mechanism by which new tunings open the door to completely new music.

DADGAD tuning is more flexible and versatile than you would imagine at a glance, and many players use it to play in key centers other than D. All tunings are a trade-off, and each has advantages and disadvantages, though it can take some time and effort to really understand them.

Droning

Probably the first thing you notice is the open-string droning and resonance. Droning is a big part of music all over the world, and is at the center of bagpipe music, where danceable melodies are played against a variety of droning pitches. (DADGAD is strongest in the key of D, which is a very common and important key for fiddle music.) In DADGAD tuning, the guitar immediately behaves more like open-tuned, droning stringed instruments like banjo and dulcimer. The kinds of sounds you get when you move melodic notes around while leaving open strings droning are hypnotic and seductive, and quite unlike the normal experience of playing guitar in standard tuning. (Unless you are playing flamenco and Spanish guitar, which make similar use of the droning E and B strings, usually played in E *Phrygian* mode. Some classical guitar composers like Sor and Tarrega also made extensive use of drone strings in the key of E, but their sound really does not work the same way as DADGAD and other open tunings.)

New Voicings

Probably the next thing you notice in DADGAD tuning is that familiar chords from standard tuning really aren't there. Even playing a pure E minor chord, probably the simplest chord in standard tuning, becomes much harder. Here are 3 ways to do it:

The droning D and A notes also add themselves easily to many chords. Many players who use tunings don't really know the names of the notes they are playing in either standard or other tunings, and may not realize how quickly we enter fresh musical territory when we use a new tuning. The truth is that you instantly have access to thousands of chords and resonances that cannot be played in standard tuning. In this book there are about 2500 chords, and about half are voicings that can be played in standard tuning, and the other half are sequences of notes that are new to our ears.

DADGAD is not hugely different from standard tuning, since only 3 strings are a whole step flat from were they usually are, so it makes sense that there is not a higher percentage of new chords available. In some other tunings and partial capo environments I have explored, many more chords are fresh voicings.

Let's look at an important chord in DADGAD tuning, a type of Gadd9 chord that is used very often as a substitute G chord. The only way to get this 1-5-1-3-2-5 voicing in standard tuning is the Aadd9 shown here:

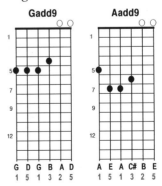

Gadd9	Aadd9
G D G B A D	A E A C# B E
1 5 1 3 2 5	1 5 1 3 2 5

A simple D chord in DADGAD is shown here with the only matching voicing in standard tuning:

3

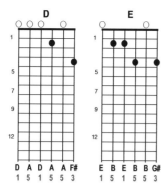

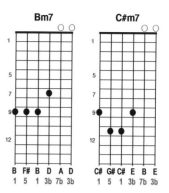

The 1-finger D5 chord that is the first thing you learn in DADGAD also has an equivalent standard tuning voicing (E5)

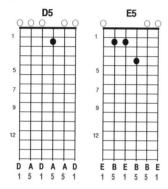

but if you move to the 7th fret and play a different D5 chord, it correlates to an unplayable 1-5-1-1-5-1 E5 chord in standard tuning:

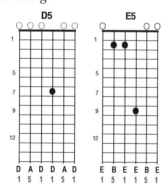

The common Bm chord form used often in DADGAD is really a Bm7, and it also has a counterpart voicing (1-5-1-3b-7b-3b) in standard tuning as a C#m7:

> *...You can't just map the chords from one tuning onto another and expect that they will match one to one.*

This Em7add11 chord we often play as a substitute Em chord in DADGAD tuning has no counterpart in standard tuning, and Mel Bay never heard this 1-5-1-3b-4-7b sequence of notes in all his years of playing guitar and making chord books. I doubt that many music theory textbooks would tell you to substitute a minor 7add11 for a regular minor chord, but that is what happens easily in DADGAD.

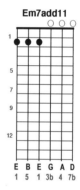

This sort of thing happens a lot in new tunings, and you can't just map the chords from one tuning onto another and expect that they will match one to one.

New Kinds of Chords

There are even new kinds of chords that appear in new tunings, often with close voicings where notes are clustered in new ways, and also harp-like chords, where the notes of a chord can be spread out across multiple strings. The fact that strings 1-2-3 are closer together in pitch in DADGAD than in standard tuning means that a number of close-voiced chords appear that don't work in standard tuning.

Here are a C6/9/11 and a D6/9/11 chord that have quite unique voicings that cannot be played in standard tuning at all. Chords like these have been lying dormant and unknown through all the millions of players exploring standard tuning. Notice that the D6/9/11 has the 1-2-3-4-5-6 scale notes in it. (These need to be arpeggiated!) It's hard to play but worth the effort.

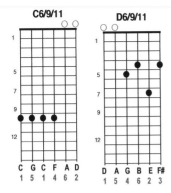

C6/9/11

C G C F A D
1 5 1 4 6 2

D6/9/11

D A G B E F#
1 5 4 6 2 3

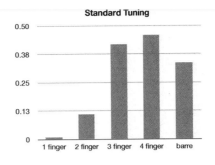

Standard Tuning

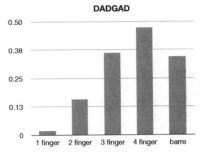

DADGAD

Comparing DADGAD to Standard

The fact that it is 7 frets between the two bottom strings but the treble strings are closer together musically means that it is fundamentally a bit different to play chords and scales in DADGAD than in standard tuning, where the strings are nearly evenly spaced. The primary consequences of this are that there are some new close-voiced chords available in DADGAD, but the scales and chords are more spread out in the bass side because the two bottom strings are 7 frets apart musically. Interestingly, the graphs of the percentages of chords that require a reach of frets 1-6 in this book and in my standard tuning complete chord book are not that different. DADGAD has a few more 1 and 2-fret chords (24% vs. 20%), but other than that there is almost no difference.

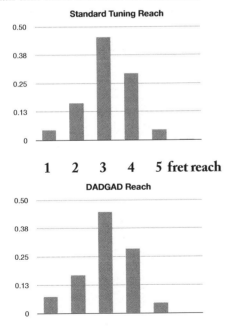

Standard Tuning Reach

1   2   3   4   5 fret reach

DADGAD Reach

Barre chords comprise 34% of the chords in both books.

In standard tuning, 1 & 2-finger chords shapes make up 12% of the chords, while in DADGAD it is 18%. There are 6% fewer 3-finger chords in DADGAD, but other than that the 2 tunings are very similar.

Substituting Chords

The droning strings that DADGAD gives us are not only useful for combining with melodies, but they add new colors to many other chords. The added 1st string D on top of an Em chord makes it into Em7, it adds a 9th to C-root chords, a flat 3rd to B chords, a 4th (or 11th) to A chords, a flat 7th to E chords, and a 6th to F chords. A big part of the sound of this tuning involves the substituting of new voicings, and for the most part, you won't be able to play familiar chords at all in DADGAD. You'll quickly learn to stop trying to get the same sounds and surrender to the new flavors of this tuning.

This underscores a drawback to chord books such as this one. If you are looking for something to use for a C chord in a song the key of D, for example, you might decide that a Cadd9, a C5, a C6/9 or C9/11 works best, and your ear is the best guide. You'll want to try a lot of fingerings to find the best one for what you are playing. You can't really apply any rulebook of music theory to tell you what substitutions are "correct."

Celtic Music

A large part of the reason that tuning has spread rapidly is that Irish, English and Scottish guitarists have found it to be ideal for playing Celtic music. Though there was a 7-string English guitar played mostly in the 1700's, like many instruments in that era, it was primarily played by upper-class people, most often women, and was tuned in an Open C tuning. Traditional Celtic music was generally passed down as unaccompanied ballads, or as fiddle or bagpipe dance melodies, and the modern role of the guitar in any of this music was unknown.

As late as the early 20th century, an "Irish singer" was usually a classically-trained male tenor (John McCormick being the best-known of these singers of that era) who sang in an operatic manner that is completely unlike the way modern Celtic singers sing. Even when the Clancy Brothers and Tommy Makem launched their version of Irish traditional music around 1960 amid the skiffle music craze, they used only standard guitar tuning in their guitar accompaniments. Likewise, Lonnie Donegan, the Corries and other early practitioners of neo-Celtic music only had the models of American folk and blues guitarists like Woody Guthrie and Leadbelly to guide them, and new tunings were barely used.

It was not until a decade or so later when British Isles guitarists began experimenting with new tunings that the modern sound of Celtic guitar began to emerge as a new way to accompany traditional music. The modal nature of much of the music caused the voicings of standard guitar chords to work poorly. This is part of the reason why the octave mandolin or "Irish bouzouki" has also become widely used in Celtic music. The open voicings of instruments tuned in 5ths work better than standard guitar chords, which always have musical 3rds.

When DADGAD showed up, there was already a problem to be solved. It took root very quickly, and Celtic guitarists immediately embraced its sound. A few more adventurous guitarists like Nic Jones and Martin Carthy developed other guitar tunings, and some players have developed "offshoots" of DADGAD, such as "Orkney" tuning (CGDGCD), CGDGAD or CGCDGA. A certain amount of experimenting is still going on.

DADGAD tuning is so widespread now in Celtic music that the use of standard tuning is disappearing, and it is common for an Irish guitarist to play only in DADGAD. Young players undoubtedly assume that the guitar styles we now use in this music have roots beyond the 1960's, since the songs and tunes themselves are often centuries old.

Modern Celtic guitarists use DADGAD to accompany songs, arrange solo instrumental guitar pieces, and also for rhythm guitar in band situations to back up fiddle and other dance music. They will often play without a capo, choosing to employ the "flavors" that the tuning imparts to keys other than D. Most Celtic music is played in D, G and A and the relative minor or modal keys, and DADGAD tuning can be effectively used in all of them.

Songwriters

In recent years singer-songwriters have also discovered DADGAD tuning, and an increasing number of guitarists who have few ties to Celtic music are also using the tuning. Jimmy Page from the band Led Zeppelin was an early adopter, as were Pink Floyd and Nick Drake, and now artists such as Marcus Mumford, Paul Simon, Jeff Tweedy, Aerosmith, Slipknot, Rory Gallagher and others make use of it. Dan Tyminski's version of *Man of Constant Sorrow* in the *O Brother Where Art Thou* movie soundtrack was also played in DADGAD, though the use of the tuning in bluegrass music is currently still rare.

The phrase "DADGAD tuning" is easy to search for on the internet, and you should not have trouble finding a long list of literally hundreds of artists of all levels and styles who use the tuning. There is no shortage of videos of guitarists playing in DADGAD.

About This and Other Guitar Chord Books

I am hoping that this chord compendium will be readable, user-friendly and accessible, as well as detailed and complete. DADGAD tuning is growing steadily more widespread, but I could not find a source that had the breadth of information that is included here. Books either show just the author's favorite handful of chords, or there are sloppily-drawn, incomplete and poorly organized charts to download off the internet. I thought it was time to lay it all out on paper of how the tuning works.

This chord book has grown out of my lifelong fascination with the complexity and diversity of guitar chords. I have been a professional acoustic guitar player my entire adult life, and now after 45 years playing guitar, I find myself probing deeper than ever into the mysteries of what make

different chords and voicings behave the way they do.

What chords you know and use are really a matter of memory more than anything, and there are limits to how much of the fingerboard geometry our brains can retain. Once you have the motor skills on both hands to form chords and strike the strings, the task of learning a new tuning is entirely one of mapping out the new possibilities, trying to understand the internal logic of the tuning, and applying it to existing or new music.

It takes a great deal of time to sort out the possibilities and opportunities each tuning offers, and it is difficult to keep track of what is happening, because of the complexity of a 6-string fingerboard, and because the note names are not in familiar places. It takes us a long time to learn where the notes are on the fingerboard, and with each new tuning, they all move around. The strategy of how the new fretboard geometry applies to the underlying chord structure and music theory is then compounded by the equally complex task of figuring out which fingers can reach what notes on what strings. So I think it makes sense to compile books of chords in various tunings rather than just memorizing all the information, watching it on internet videos or trying to keep it in a phone.

I built this library of chords amid a multi-year project to explore more carefully the new opportunities offered by partial capos. The more I dug into the fingerboard, the more diversity and complexity I found, and I am a bit in awe of all the different ways I have found to play every kind of chord. In my chord research I have built a library of chords that now contains nearly 20,000 fingerings in dozens of different tunings. I am sure that I am still by no means exhausting all the possibilities offered by 6 strings and 4 fingers.

By sifting through my database, I have been able to determine just how many times a given chord voicing is repeated in the list, and which ones are rare or unique. The results have been surprising. A significant percentage of all those thousands of chords are voicings that only show up once, so instead of finding the same chords over and over again, I instead get an exciting variety of ways to scramble the note order in chords, each with a unique sound.

It seems to be pretty typical for a common chord, especially one with some open strings, to show up in 20 to 40 forms in a given tuning. If you pull back and see what happens on a bigger scale, you'll find that an E chord, for example, can be played on a 6-string instrument strung with normal strings in about 150-200 unique ways that have musical value to a guitarist. (About 20 of them are playable in standard tuning.) It's my ball-park estimate that any given tuning lets us play only about 1/6 of the possible voicings that the guitar allows, so by sticking to a single tuning, you will miss out on the other 5/6 of possible fingerings that are simply not playable in your chosen tuning.

The list of A major chords at the beginning of this book, for example, shows 25 ways to make sure that all the strings ringing are sounding an A, C# or E note. That seems like a lot, since some "chord bible" publications show only two or three A major chords. My chord database now numbers over 125 distinct ways to voice an A chord, without including the really useless ones that have multiple C#'s on the bottom, for example. I have become increasingly fascinated with how many total possibilities there are, and how much diversity and complexity can come from even something like a simple major or minor chord, with just 3 notes occupying the guitar landscape.

I have also become increasingly intrigued with the decisions, strategies and possibilities that arise from the trying to play a certain group of notes on a 6-string fingerboard. Finding as many fingerings as possible, and trying to determine which ones were both playable and musical became a pastime. After countless hours of studying chords and logging the results, my conclusions surprised me.

There are far more ways to play and voice guitar chords than we realize. The A7, A9 and A6/9 chords are near the top of the list in standard tuning, and A7 and Dm win in this book, with 63 and 60 entries. There is sometimes just no reasonable way at all to play a sequence of notes, such as a Bmaj9 chord, and other chords may only offer a few options. Some keys favor certain types of chord, and obviously DADGAD tuning favors chords in the D-root family, with the nice 1-5 open strings on the low end allowing all sorts of extensions to be added on the treble side. DADGAD does well with "modal" chords, with no 3rds, and standard tuning doesn't. DADGAD does poorly with minor 11ths and 13ths.

It's hard to tell by glancing at this book what is not here, nor is it easy to simply imagine what you can get from other tunings. Some of my other guitar chord books unveil thousands of new chords I have found in my explorations. This should be very exciting to composers, songwriters and arrangers who are looking for fresh sounds. The newly-available music is the reason that so many players are exploring alternate tunings, but because the guitar education world still remains inextricably tied to standard tuning, I have never seen a scholarly discussion of the musical possibilities that altered tunings

> **All the chords in this book are playable, and they have all been "hand-tested" and are not generated with software merely cranking out permutations of notes.**
>
> **The chords and voicings were optimized for solo and acoustic guitarists, and most have 5 or 6 strings sounding. Both open-string and barre chord forms are included.**

or partial capos present.

Self-taught, non-sight-reading, "un-schooled" guitarists all over the world are generating huge amounts of interesting and fresh guitar music in hundreds of tunings, yet the guitar education books and classes often go on as if this other body of guitar music did not exist.

There are literally hundreds of non-standard tunings that have been used throughout history, and each of them offers a unique set of possibilities, and a new set of chord and scale fingerings. Each tuning presents a new set of trade-offs, where you lose access to some things and gain others. Some players choose to spend their entire careers playing in one non-standard tuning, though it is more common for guitar players seem to dabble in various tunings without making a total commitment to just one.

Likewise, each way to put a partial capo on a guitar opens some doors and closes others, and it is a delicate and difficult task to try them all and find the ones that offer the most new music. (This is the goal of my extensive series of *Capo Voodoo* books.) Some of the most fruitful fingerboard environments I have found involve combining different tunings with partial capos, and in

some of them, over 90% of the chords I have logged are new chords and voicings. I am in the midst of building a number of other chord books to chart the terrain in many of these new partial capo configurations. As a result of my chord research, I now have "scientific" evidence that there are indeed significant numbers of fascinating new combinations of notes available that not even the best players on earth have ever been able to play before without switching tunings, adding partial capos, or both. The guitar fingerboard, with your 4 fingers accessing the 6 strings across 12 to 15 frets, is much deeper and contains more surprises than any of us can really wrap our minds around.

Recently I have also found a way to "map" guitar chords onto the piano keyboard to see visually where the notes lie, and have been quite surprised by the results of that also. Since I don't play the piano, I always assumed that with 10 fingers and two hands there can't be much on a guitar fingerboard that can't be duplicated on a keyboard. With notes in 4 octaves on the guitar, I have indeed found a significant number of guitar chord voicings that are not "reachable" on the piano.

What's In This Book

This chord book is tailored to the needs of the "troubadour guitarist," who most often plays an acoustic instrument, where open-string chords are very common. Included here are a mixture of open and closed voicings, though this is by no means a "Mel Bay style" jazz guitar book for DADGAD tuning. In fact, I have kept the book a lot shorter by leaving out jazz chords. The whole sound of what we know as "jazz guitar" is built around the voicings of standard tuning, and though DADGAD players are getting more adventurous all the time and using more complex chords, there is no pressing need as yet for a DADGAD jazz guitar book. After decades of evolution, so-called "jazz guitar" does not appear poised to embrace the new possibilities of DADGAD tuning in the foreseeable future.

Even if you don't just strum chords, and play more linear or complex instrumental music, the left-hand positions as shown in this book are really the starting point for understanding how a tuning works. A striking or appealing chord voicing in this book could easily be the starting point for a song accompaniment or an instrumental piece, and players of all levels commonly think in terms of putting their fingers in a particular place on the guitar, thus creating a "chord shape." Even

when we play single-note guitar music, we usually don't just have one finger on the fingerboard at a time, and scales and melodies constantly thread themselves through chord shapes all across the fingerboard.

It's one thing to play a chord that "fits" in a band arrangement, but solo guitarists need the best possible chord with the fullest sound, because there is no band or bass player.

Chord books for "folk guitar" tend to be incomplete and simplistic, and don't even hint at the depth and complexity of the guitar fingerboard or all the musical options. There is a surprising amount of diversity in the voicings and fingerings of any kind of chord, including the simplest ones, and every guitarist will benefit from fingerboard and chord theory.

Modal Chords

Nearly all skilled troubadours make some use of the simple "modal" or "power" chord (that is technically not even a chord, since it has only 2 notes in it) that is just a root and a fifth with no third, commonly written with a numeral 5 as the suffix. Modal chords are musically powerful and widely used, and deserve a place in a chord book.

The D5 chord is extremely important in DADGAD tuning, and there are 26 of them shown here. Jazz-oriented chord books generally omit this chord entirely as if it did not exist. There are no movable barre versions of this chord in standard tuning, and you can only play a few A5, C5, D5 G5, or E5 chords. Modal chords are easy in DADGAD tuning, which may be yet another reason why the tuning has caught on so well in folk and traditional music.

I also gave a distinct name to major "chords" that have no 5th, and you will see some A3 and D3 chords here, though technically they are not really chords. There is even one voicing of a D1 "chord" where all 6 strings sound a D note (p.66).

Similarly, other chord books even sometimes ignore the suspended 4th chord, where the musical 3rd is replaced by a 4th. Troubadours use this chord constantly, regardless of whether music professors consider it a legitimate "triad." The open strings in DADGAD form a suspended 4th chord.

The notes that make up any chord can be in different orders, and some notes may be repeated (doubled) or missing. The ways the notes combine and react with each other musically, due to their positions in the chord, are endlessly interesting and subtle.

Even when we play single-note guitar music, we usually don't just have one finger on the fingerboard at a time, and scales and melodies constantly thread themselves through chord shapes all across the fingerboard.

The whole fingerboard is shown for each chord, making it much easier to identify and use chords.

You can visually see the "logic" of a chord as you scan all the ways to play it. You can't see this at all on 5-fret diagrams the way other chord books show them.

Possibly the most important feature in this book is that the letter names and musical function of every note in every chord are shown. This is a wonderful theory lesson, and allows you to see the voicing and structure of every chord.

All the chords in this book are playable, and they have all been "hand-tested" and are not generated with software merely cranking out permutations of notes. Some of them are very difficult. Like dictionaries of words, choices had to be made about what to include and leave out. There is no substitute for taking time to carefully try each chord fingering, and I have done that for you in this book.

Why do you even need different ways to play chords?
Probably the most important reason is when you are playing a solo guitar arrangement of a song or instrumental piece. Most solo troubadours like to keep as many strings ringing as possible to keep a full sound, and most of us will work very hard to have a bass string sounding underneath and supporting whatever else we are doing. When we don't have a bass player or a band, we generally need to keep as much rhythm, harmony, melody and bass going all at once as we can. As the melody of a song moves around or changes octaves, it often requires us to switch voicings of the chord to keep the song flowing.

We also need both open and closed-position voicings of chords so we can either let open strings ring and resonate, or if we want to play more staccato, bouncier rhythm changes, which require barre chords.

Another vital reason to know multiple voicings of a chord is that often a particular chord voicing has a sound that the others don't. So many classic songs have been built around the sound of a specific guitar chord, and there are still chords out there that no one has made into a memorable guitar part. Maybe you will find one here, since the reachable chords in standard tuning have been picked over for centuries by millions of players.

A final reason to know many ways to play a chord is that if you are playing with another guitarist, it usually sounds better if you play different versions of the chord, often on different parts of the fingerboard where the tone is also different. A lot of famous artists (*The Rolling Stones* and *The Allman Brothers* are good examples) have built a distinctive sound around the way two guitars play together.

Please relax about names of chords. There are no "official names" for chords, and people use different symbols and abbreviations, like dialects of language. You will often see a capital M7 for major 7th, an add2 or sus2 for an add9, sus for sus4, add4 for add11, etc. A minus sign is often used for minor. I used *Adim* in this book for diminished because there is no convenient typographic symbol in my publishing software for A^0, with the superscript zero, a common symbol used for this chord.

Some chords have special names and other types don't.

It's not uncommon for the same group of notes to have more than one name. The most common example of this is that a minor 7th chord has the same notes as a 6th chord. (Am7= A C E G and C6= C E G A, for example.) Minor 9th chords are often the same notes as major 7th chords, and I have sometimes included both.

Many chords in chord books are difficult or nearly impossible to finger. My rule was that I did not include a chord that I would not personally use in a song or instrumental piece. I have a good left hand, and if I can't play it, I left it out of this book. We can't just use computers to choose chords: humans have to make decisions, and I rejected a lot of chords that I thought were unreasonably hard to play. I sometimes wish I could have put some kind of a difficulty index into this book, since some chords are vastly harder than others. (This is of course subjective, and different players favor different kinds of shapes.) It would be fun to make a guitar chord book for professional basketball players, since their hands are so much larger than most of ours.

I thought long and hard about barre chord symbols. All players don't make the same decisions about whether to use a barre or partial barre, and it is not that hard to find the fingering that is best for you. If there are more than 4 dots on the fingerboard, it's a sign that there are some barred notes.

There are a lot of "gray areas" in naming and discussing chords. A group of notes can function as more than one chord, depending on which note is the root, and how it is used in the context of a song. You may not agree with my choices, and you may find the same chord shape with more than one name in this book. This is a big part of the reason I did the work to include the note names of every chord.

Augmented & diminished chords take up a lot of space. There are many ways to play these chords, though there are a lot of muted (x) strings. Each has multiple names and they have a lot of useful and nearly equivalent inversions, so they take up a lot of room in a book like this, though troubadours don't use them often. They are important, so they were included, though they tend to be awkward to finger, and neither of them fit well on the guitar in common tunings. They are commonly used as "passing" or "transitional" chords, and you don't usually strum them.

It's unclear what to do about "slash" chords. These are often notated as a slash followed by a letter, such as C/A. This means play a C chord, but with an A bass note. It is a rather common thing that guitarists do: a lot of well-known songs such as *Mr. Bojangles* or *Friend of the Devil* feature a moving bass, usually starting on the 1 bass note. The bass notes start with C on the A string and descend down. You are not really strumming a chord with a B and then an A root– as a player you are thinking that you are holding a C chord and just doing a walkdown on the lower strings. The effect is really not as if you are strumming discrete chords. The slash notation allows us to describe what is going on without trying to invent names for a C chord with a B bass, followed by a C chord with an A bass, and so on. A number of these kinds of passing chords are useful and beautiful, but they don't work well in a "snapshot gallery" of chords like this book.

The slash followed by a number, such as 6/9 or 9/11, means that the chord has more than one "added tone." A Cadd9 chord has C-E-G-D and a Cadd11 has C-E-G-F. The C 9/11 chord is C-E-G-D-F, which you could call add9/add11 or add9/11.

What's Not In This Book

Obviously, this kind of book is bound to have some errors and omissions, so the chords that I neglected to put in are not here. Hopefully they are few and not really important ones...

Left-hand finger numbers are not shown here because not everyone plays every chord the same way. The truth is, if you play guitar, you will constantly be learning new fingerings, so get used to always changing. You'll be a better player if you can learn to use alternate fingerings whenever it makes sense.

Muted-note duplicates. If you play a 6-string chord, and mute one or more of the strings, it sort of becomes a different chord. I decided it would be "overkill" to include multiple versions of every chord shape in this book where the only differences between them is a muted string. When a mute string causes you to change the fingering strategy, I may have included it as a new chord.

When you move a closed shape up the neck, it also makes sense that when it forms a C#root chord you would mute the bass D string, but when you move it a half step higher and it forms a D-root chord, you let the bass string ring, because anybody would do that. Computer-generated chord lists are often not "smart" enough to accommodate situations like these.

Unplayable chords. If I can't play the chord, I left it out. Here is an example of an obvious chord that is in many collections of DADGAD chords, but I can't figure out how to play it.

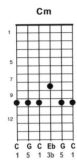

Cm

C G C Eb G C
1 5 1 3b 5 1

There are no double sharps or double flats. There are valid musical reasons for using double accidentals, but there is physically no room for them in my chord diagrams, and they are confusing, so I vetoed them. This book is designed for people who don't have degrees in music theory. It's hard enough to tell people that the 4th fret of the 1st string in DADGAD tuning is sometimes called F# and sometimes a Gb. To insist that an A note is sometimes a G## and sometimes a Bbb is being a little too rigorous. If you know enough music theory to be bothered by the lack of double accidentals then you should understand what is going on and not be bothered. The purpose of the book is to show you a lot of chords and choices for chords, and what notes are in them.

Here is how double flats can occur: diminished chords are technically triads, with just 3 notes in them, but they are almost always played on guitar as four-note diminished 7th chords, with three minor 3rds stacked up instead of 2. The Cdim chords in every guitar book in the world have an A note along with the C-Eb-Gb diminished triad. I have "illegally"called it an A, since "technically" it should be called a Bbb. Diminished chords are unusual, and each one has 4 names, and the notes in them get renamed if you give the chord a different name. The key is A, which has the 6th note of F#, but the "rules" say the note in the chord has to be called a Gb. The Fdim chord here shows a 6th scale degree = D note, which technically should be an Ebb, and a 7bb.

This kind of situation is an example of terminology and explanations that become more obscure as they try to be more clear. It happens in pronunciation and grammar also. We follow rules to avoid doing things like ending sentences with prepositions, and we end up saying things like "*That is something up with which I shall not put.*"

A prominent web discussion on *Yahoo.com* said this to "explain" the apparent A note when someone asked why there is an A in a Cdim chord: "*The distance from C to B is a Major 7th. The distance from C to Bb is a minor 7th. The distance from C to Bbb is a diminished 7th. In no way is it a 6th. That would be from a C of some sort up to an A of some*

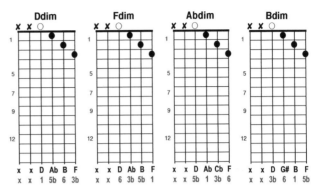

Ddim	Fdim	Abdim	Bdim
x x ○	x x ○	x x ○	x x ○

		Ddim			Fdim			Abdim			Bdim
x	x	D Ab B F	x	x	D Ab B F	x	x	D Ab Cb F	x	x	D G# B F
x	x	1 5b 6 3b	x	x	6 3b 5b 1	x	x	5b 1 3b 6	x	x	3b 6 1 5b

sort. There is a logic to our theoretical terminology. There are many things implied in the spelling of a chord, not the least of which is actual intonation. A and Bbb are NOT the same pitch. Another implication is one of voice leading. And there is the question as to what the root of the chord is. Spelled the proper way, the root is C. Spelled your way the root becomes A. Then it would be an A diminished 7th. (A C Eb Gb) Are you then going to insist that the Gb be respelled as an F#?? Oops -- then we have an F# diminished 7th -- F# A C Eb -"

I am not sure this clarifies anything. Likewise a C# augmented (+) chord would have the notes C# E# G##, which if rigorously enforced, would indeed mean that we would have to tell troubadours to be ready to call an F# a Gb, and that they should also be ready to call a G an Abb or an F##. To us guitar players, the G string is the G string, it's not the F## string sometimes. In this book, you'll see the C#+ chords incorrectly show an F and not an E#, and an A instead of the G##. My apologies.

Speaking of rules, the system of rules that says that we must accept double flats and sharps also says that you are not supposed to use parallel 5ths, 4ths or octaves in harmony. Every guitar player on Earth who can play barre chords has played this chord progression in standard tuning:

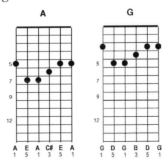

A	G

A E A C# E A
1 5 1 3 5 1

G D G B D G
1 5 1 3 5 1

It's rife with parallel 5ths, 4ths and octaves. So what? It's something guitarists do. Just because pianists don't do that (and probably can't even play these chords) doesn't mean we can't. Who says it's breaking rules? Just because pianists developed this language and notation doesn't really give them permanent license to make and enforce rules that really don't make sense to guitarists.

There are no warnings here telling you not to use your thumb to fret notes on the guitar. I'd like to go on record as saying in print that it is fine to use your thumb. It's almost some kind of inside joke or conspiracy among guitar teachers, like the police who won't tell you it's OK to go over the speed limit, though we know they will let us to some extent. Virtually all guitarists use their thumbs at times, and good players go back and forth as often as they need to. Some chords are hard to play unless your thumb can hang over the bass end. Almost all players use their thumb to mute the bass E string on a D major chord, and most of them actually fret the 2nd fret F# also. This A major chord is one that you can only play if your hand and guitar neck allow you to hang the thumb over on the bass string:

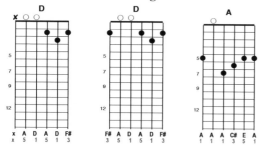

I have a collection of guitar instruction books, and only one of them, an old jazz guitar book by Gene Leis, contains a photograph of someone with their thumb prominently hanging over the fingerboard. Many guitar instruction books have strongly worded warnings against using the thumb. The truth is that when your thumb is over the edge of the fingerboard, it greatly limits the reach you have with your 4th finger. If you need to stretch a long way across the fingerboard, put your thumb in back. If you need to use your thumb, use it and quit worrying. Sometimes it is needed to fret 2 or even 3 bass strings.

I left out a lot of chord types that are associated only with jazz. For example, the book would have been nearly twice as long if I had included these: *b5, augmented 7th, augmented 9th, 7 flat5, 9 flat5, 9#11, 7#9, 7 b9, 13b9, 13b5, minor 7 flat5, b7b9, minor 9 flat5, minor-major 7th, minor major 9th, b13b9, 13b5b9, 13b5b9, 11b9.* There are a few scattered extended chords that I liked and included, like #1746 and #1748.

I even left out the *minor-major 7th*: 1-3b-5-7 that you learn about in any music theory curriculum. Structurally this chord is pretty simple, since it has the flat 3rd and the unflatted 7th notes, but it is pretty dissonant and hard to use in campfire-style guitar. Here is an "A minor major 7th" chord, also written as mM7, mΔ7, -Δ7, mM7, m/M7, m(M7), minmaj7, m⑦

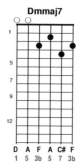

The Beatles used this kind of chord in *Magical Mystery Tour,* and *Pink Floyd* used it in *Us and Them.* (It is sometimes called the "Hitchcock chord" because it was used effectively by composer Bernard Herrmann in the horror movie *Psycho.*) A handful of songs use them, but hundreds of millions of songs use major, minor and 7th chords, so I made the executive decision to leave the minor major 7th out of this book. This was done by conscious choice and not ignorance of their existence.

Things Like the "Tristan Chord" Music theorists have written long treatises on the dissonant "Tristan" chord that Wagner began his opera *Tristan & Isolde* with in 1865. It has a spelling of 1-3b-5b-7b, which isn't that different from a standard minor 7th chord, but seems to defy normal music theory explanations. (Wagner's exact notes were actually: F-B-D#-G#.) It is credited with things like triggering the onset of the 20th century atonality movement. It is not a "troubadour chord" so I have left most of them out, like quite a number of other kinds of odd or unusual chords that we really don't use much in the real world.

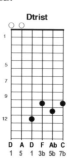

It's not hard to play this example, since Tristan chords have a reasonably easy movable fingering in DADGAD. (There is no movable form in standard tuning.) However, it's not likely you'll use one in a song. This example highlights one of the problems of making a guitar chord book. The famous *Neapolitan* chord that Beethoven and other composers used is also not a troubadour chord, and is not in this book, though you can read extensively about it on the internet if you like.

There is nothing in the chord-naming systems to indicate if notes are doubled (repeated) or omitted. An 11th chord may or may not have a 7th or 9th in it, for example, and though technically something like a 6th chord is an "extension" of a major chord, and should have 1-3-5-6 scale notes, you will find voicings that are missing the 3rd or 5th. This is part of the way guitar works, and part of what gives each voicing its own sound. The only way to know what is going on inside each chord is to listen carefully and study the letters and numbers for every chord.

A modal 7th chord, which is important in blues guitar, has no common name, and is generally just put in the pile with the other 7th chords, even though it has no 3rd, and has just the 1-5-7b notes. You'll have to study the small scale degree numbers under the chords to find these. (To my ears, Big Joe Williams' classic song *"Baby Please Don't Go"* doesn't sound right to me unless you use one.) Similarly, an augmented chord with no 3rd is just 1 and 5# notes. If you don't call it an augmented chord, then it really has no name. It's not really just an interval when there are 4 or 5 strings ringing in it.

This book doesn't use the open circle symbol to show an optional fingering. It's a common and useful thing to do, but it interferes with the way the letter names and the scale degrees of every note are shown under each chord in this book. (You can't really show the note names and the scale degrees for the optional fingerings.) A chord diagram with several open circles is more of a puzzle than a chord, and it is not simple to extract the usable fingerings.

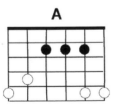

This chord diagram appears in the well-known Ted Green *"Chord Chemistry"* book, and seems to say a lot about the different ways to play an A major chord at fret 2 in standard tuning. It might be very informative and helpful, but it might also be as confusing as it is helpful. It actually parses down to 12 different fingerings that take some effort to extract from the diagram. Since you can only play one of them at a time, here are the 8 playable

choices one at a time.

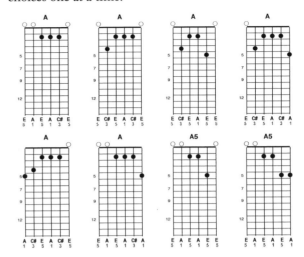

Here are the four I left out of my standard tuning book. They are playable by some of us, but impractical:

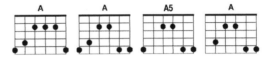

Ted Green's diagram might better represent how a skilled guitarist conceptualizes a nut position A chord, and it might not.

To illustrate how to play D chords, you could also just show the whole fingerboard of D-F#-A notes, which is also what a skilled guitarist "sees" on the fingerboard to represent a D chord in DADGAD tuning:

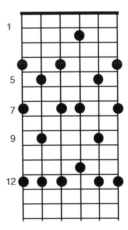

Again, this is more of a puzzle than a chord chart, and though all possible D chords in DADGAD are encoded here, the diagram is of questionable value to someone who wants to learn the different ways to play a D chord. This the kind of information that computer-generated chord charts and apps give you, but I don't think there is any substitute for a human editor who makes decisions about what chords don't sound good or are too hard to finger. I chose to show you nearly 60 distinct chord shapes represented by this chart instead of just this diagram. It takes quite a bit of effort to locate them all, and even more to actually know them and be able to use them.

Arpeggiated Chords

The Italian word *arpeggio* literally means "broken chord" and the choice of whether the notes in a chord are played all at once or in staggered time can make a world of difference in the sound of the chord.

For example, we fingerpickers love chords like those that I call 9/11 chords, which have the added 11th (which is the same as the 4th) and the 9th, which is shown as a 2. An A9/11 would have the A-C#-E triad with D and B added to it. This really means that you now have 1-2-3-4-5 scale notes all in the same chord, which can sound dissonant when strummed, yet haunting and harp-like when arpeggiated.

Before you decide that a chord in this book is "no good," make sure you play it forward and backwards in arpeggio, and also in a strummed form. Many of them really come to life when they are arpeggiated.

How Many Chords is Best?

Many readers who are opening this book are beginners and intermediate players, and the question arises as to whether it is better to include more or fewer chords, or perhaps to draw some lines in terms of difficulty or complexity.

If you have a lot of chords, you inevitably include "not-so-great" voicings and very difficult fingerings along with the easier and good-sounding chords. Is it perhaps better to just have the most vital and most common chords? In the spirit of "do-it-yourself," I decided to include a lot of choices of ways to play more common chords, and to not include more "obscure" types of chords. I don't think it hurts anyone to have a chord book with a lot of choices, any more than it hurts to have a dictionary with words in it than most of us will never really use.

There are issues of what is hard or easy, and also what is common or useful. If you like dissonant music, then what is a useful chord to you is not the same as it would be for someone who had more mainstream tastes and who liked consonance. Our tastes change as we get older also, and as we have life experiences. I had to make a lot of tough decisions about what chords to include, and I might have put in a chord on a day when I was feeling generous, and I may have tossed some out on other days when I was feeling differently.

A guitar chord book is somewhat of an artistic statement, and reflects the personality as well as the musical tastes and skills of the author. I hope you like this one. I really had a lot of fun making it, and it really stirred up in me a constant and ever-deepening sense of awe at all the things a we can do with our 6 strings, 4 fingers and a thumb.

In this digital world, with an endless torrent of new gadgets, software, and new interfaces, there is something profoundly satisfying about focusing entirely on a centuries-old thing like a guitar fingerboard.

If you have a lot of chords, you inevitably include "not-so-great" voicings and very difficult fingerings along with the easier and best-sounding chords.

Have fun exploring...

About the Diagrams in This Book

Some guitars have a lot more frets than others, and it's unclear how high to go up the fingerboard when you make a chord book. The note at the 12th fret is the same letter name as the open string and the fingerboard starts repeating at that point. Modern acoustic guitars generally have 14 frets to the body,

so the chord diagrams in this book go up to fret 14. If you have an electric guitar or a double cutaway you will have access to some other chord fingerings in the higher frets that are not in this book.

Open Strings - in this case the only open string is on the 2nd string

Mute String marked with x. Don't play it. Mute with left or right hand.

ID Number - Within the context of this book, each chord is assigned a number to help you keep track of them better. There is no musical meaning. This is the 11th chord in this book.

Regular Fretted Note is a black circle. Left hand fingers are not shown in this book, and I don't use the commonly-used open circle symbol for optional fingerings (because the letter names & scale degrees are shown for every chord.)

Whole Fingerboard Shown I chose to use more paper and ink to make it much easier to keep track of where the chord is on the neck and to see the musical geometry involved, rather than just show the part of the neck where the chord is, as guitar books always do.

Letter Names for all the notes in the chord. This helps immensely in understanding what is going on inside the chord.

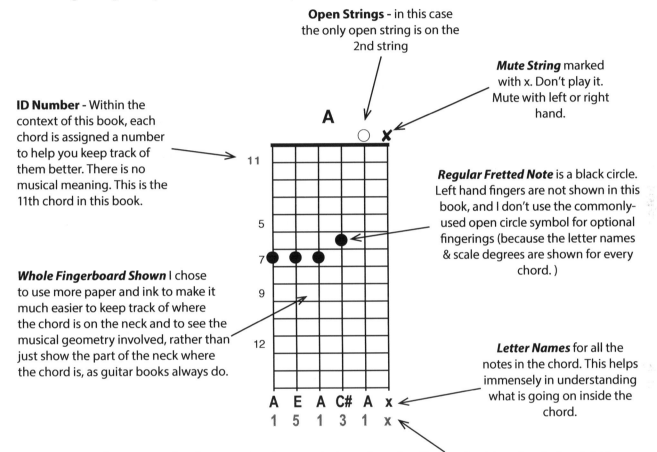

Scale Degrees of each note-- showing you the inversions, "*spelling*" and *voicing* of each chord. A big part of what gives each chord its musical identity is determined by which numbers are present. The order in which they appear, and which of them are absent or *doubled* (repeated) is also a vital factor. There are many voicings of any chord, and only a limited number of them are available on a guitar.

In this example, A is the root or 1, so the 3rd of that scale is the C#, the 5th of an A scale is E. These numbers show you the structure and help you analyze and understand the sound of each chord.

Sorting The chords in this book are sorted by root note first, and then by chord type, fret position and number of fingers in the chord. A 3-finger chord that starts at fret 4 will appear before a 3 finger barre chord at that same fret position. In a few instances I have moved a very common voicing to the front. Instead of trying to sort chord types by complexity, I put them in order of how often we use them. This is both helpful and frustrating, since it's hard to know if a minor 6th is more useful than a major 9th.

The DADGAD Tuning Fingerboard

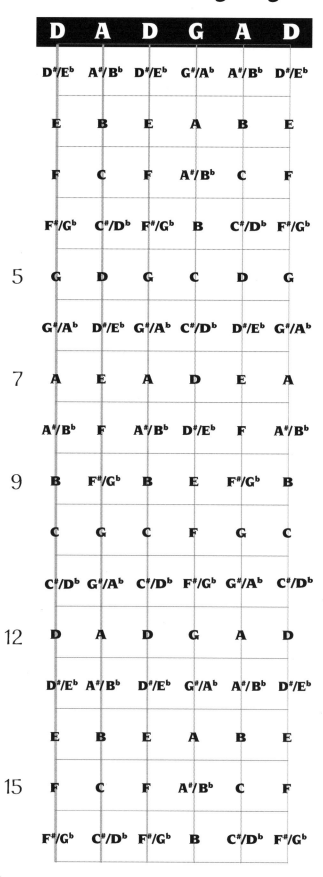

DADGAD Guitar Chords
TUNING: DADGAD

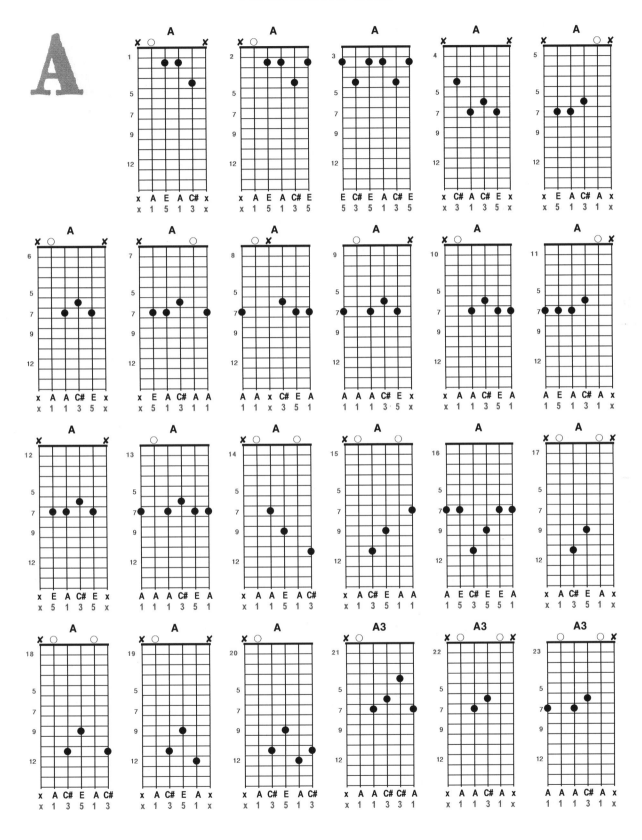

DADGAD Guitar Chords
TUNING: D A D G A D

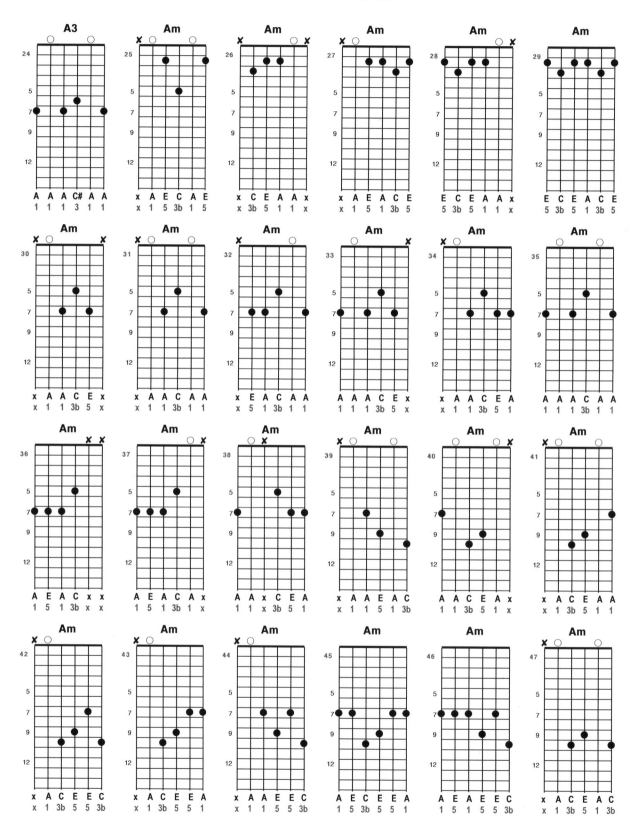

DADGAD Guitar Chords
TUNING: D A D G A D

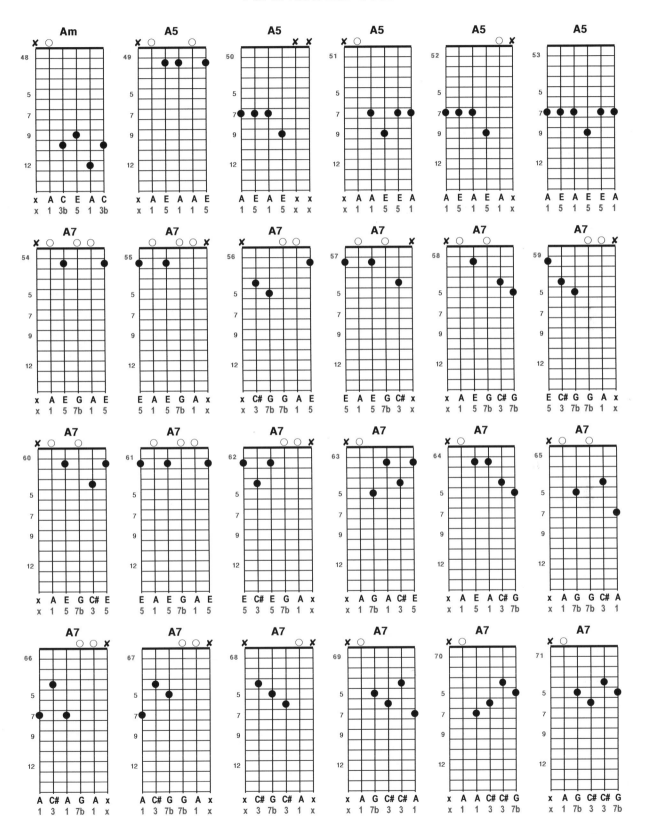

DADGAD Guitar Chords
TUNING: D A D G A D

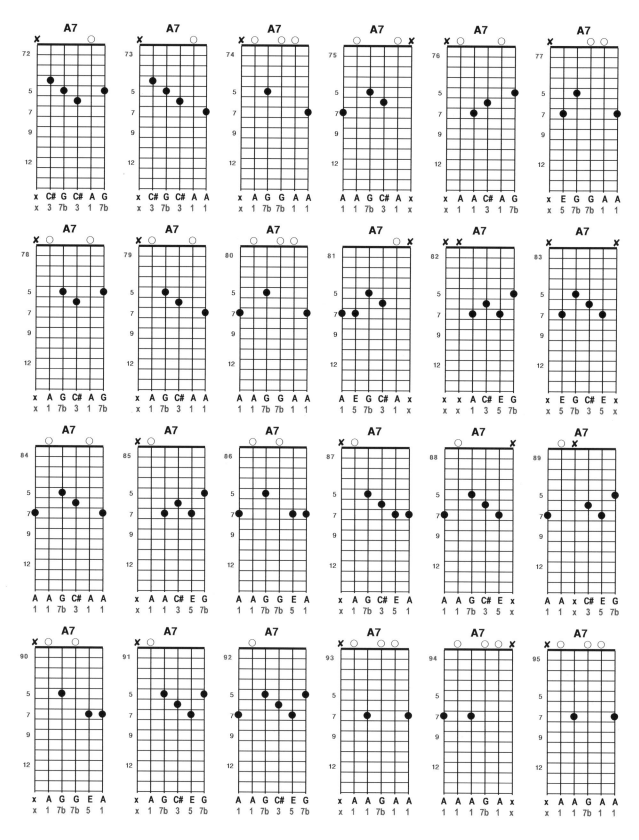

DADGAD Guitar Chords
TUNING: D A D G A D

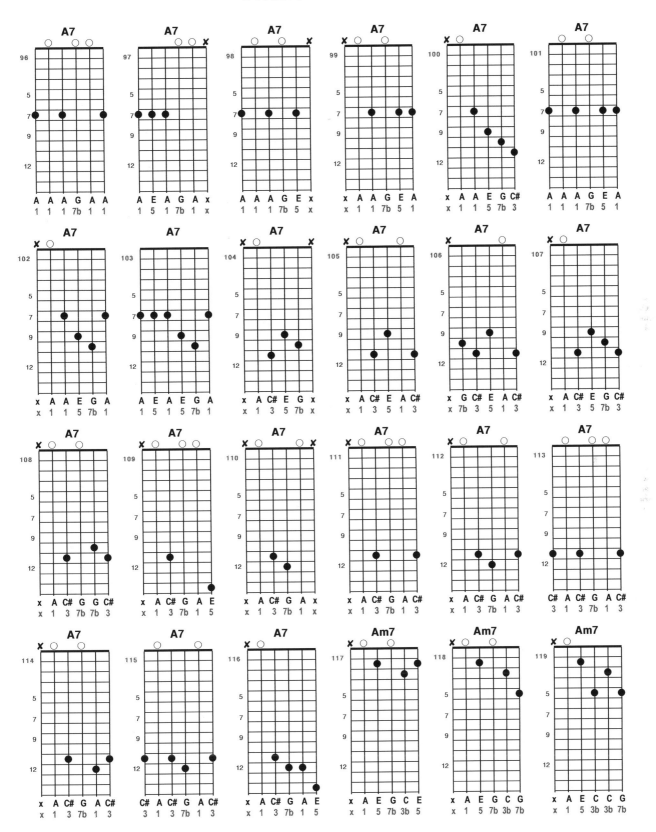

DADGAD Guitar Chords
TUNING: D A D G A D

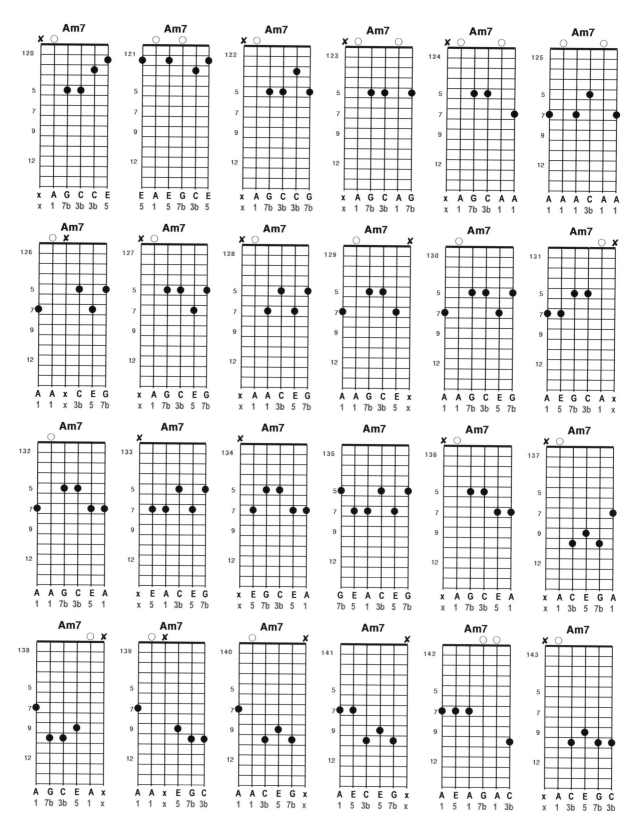

22

DADGAD Guitar Chords
TUNING: D A D G A D

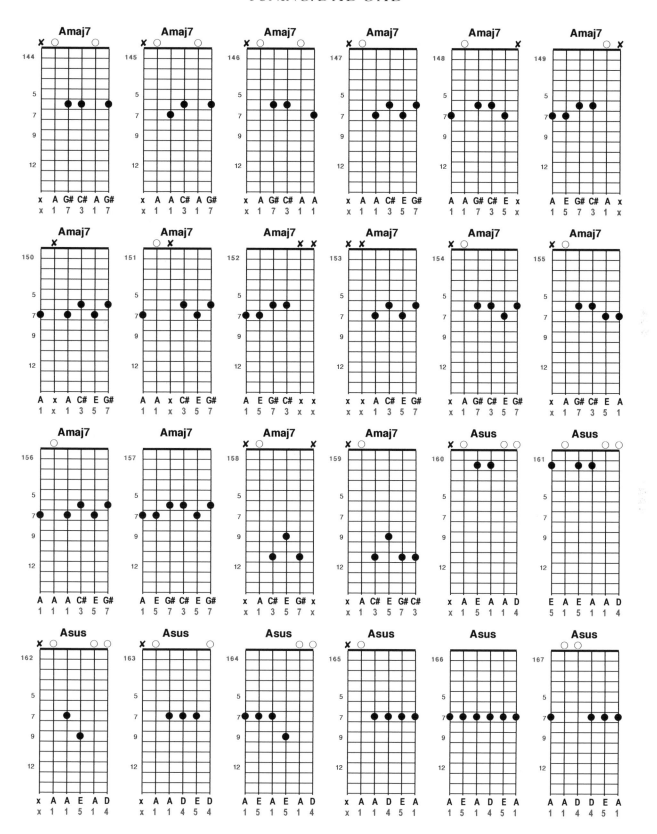

DADGAD Guitar Chords
TUNING: D A D G A D

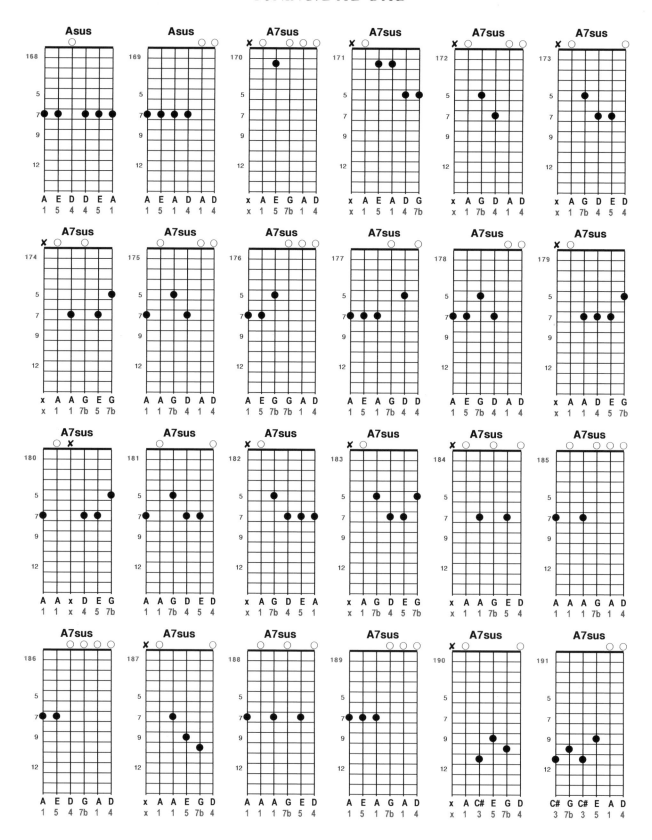

DADGAD Guitar Chords
TUNING: D A D G A D

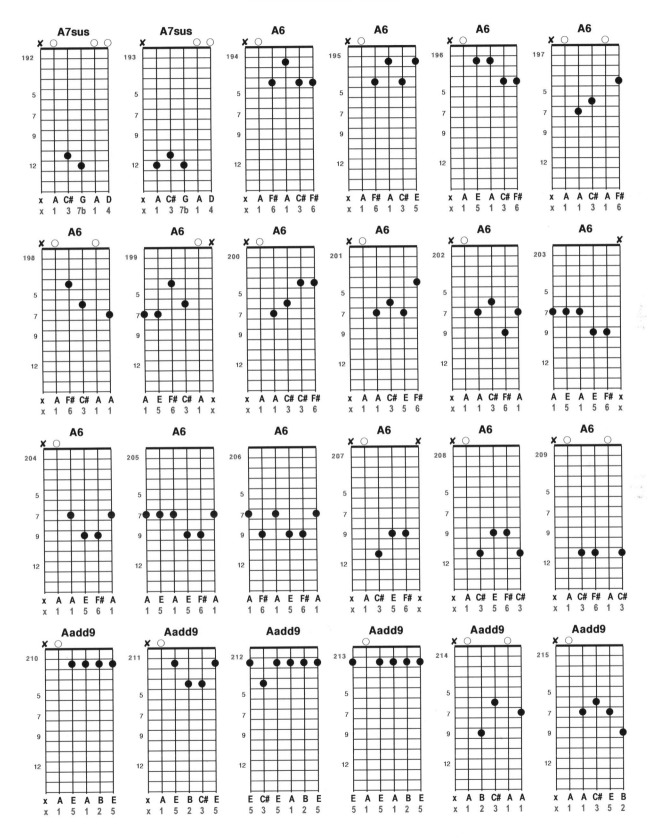

DADGAD Guitar Chords
TUNING: D A D G A D

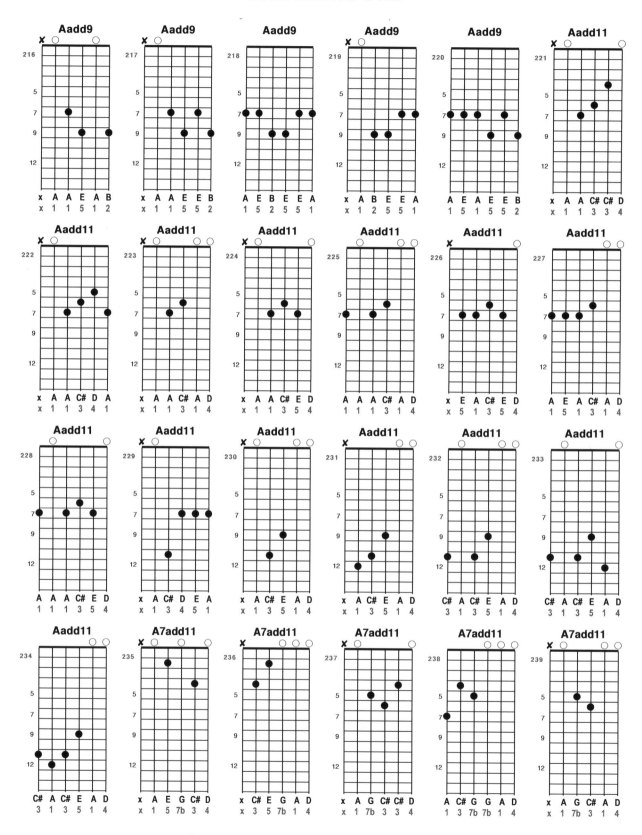

DADGAD Guitar Chords
TUNING: D A D G A D

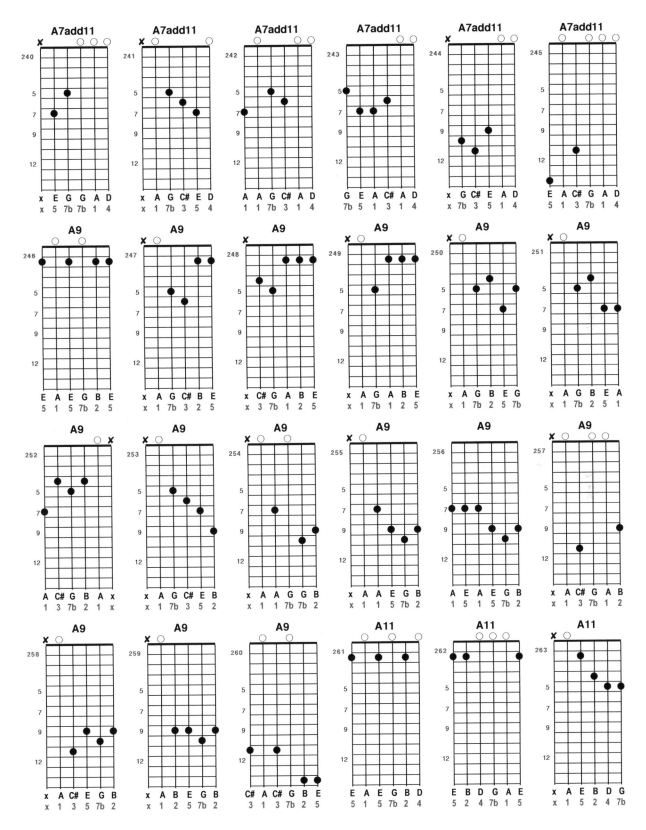

DADGAD Guitar Chords
TUNING: D A D G A D

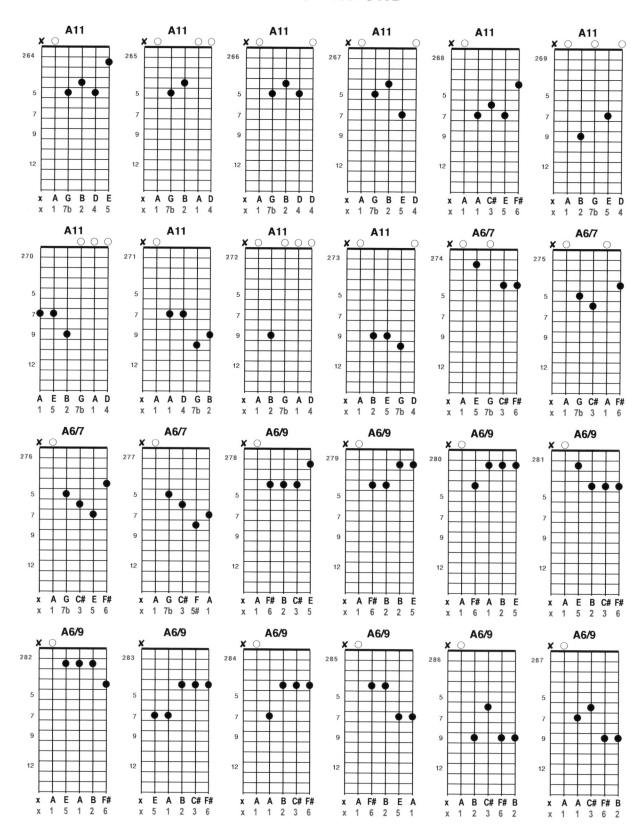

28

DADGAD Guitar Chords

TUNING: D A D G A D

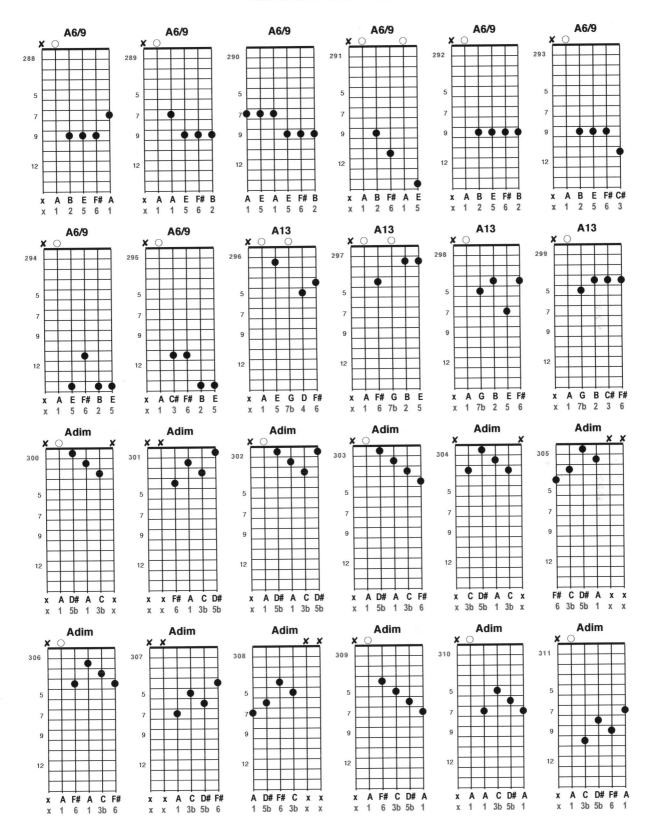

29

DADGAD Guitar Chords
TUNING: DADGAD

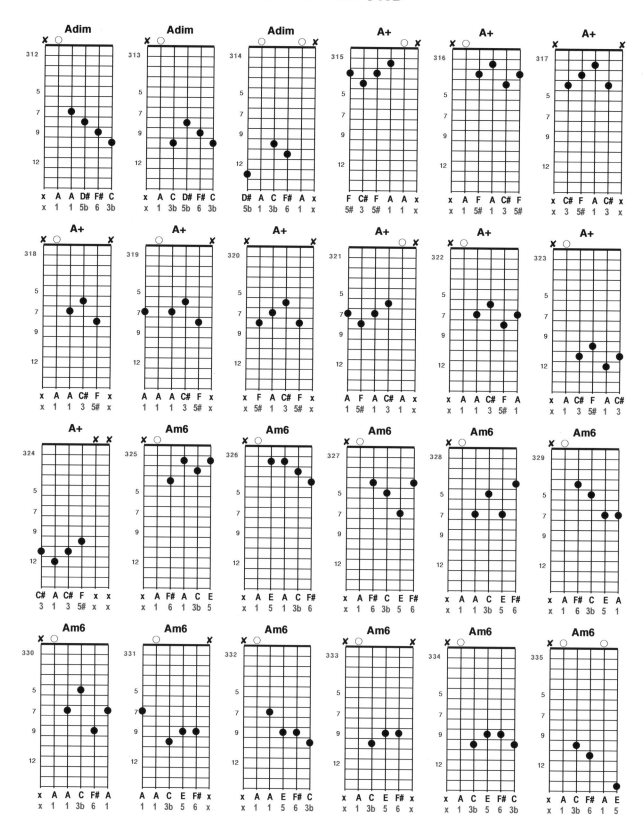

DADGAD Guitar Chords
TUNING: D A D G A D

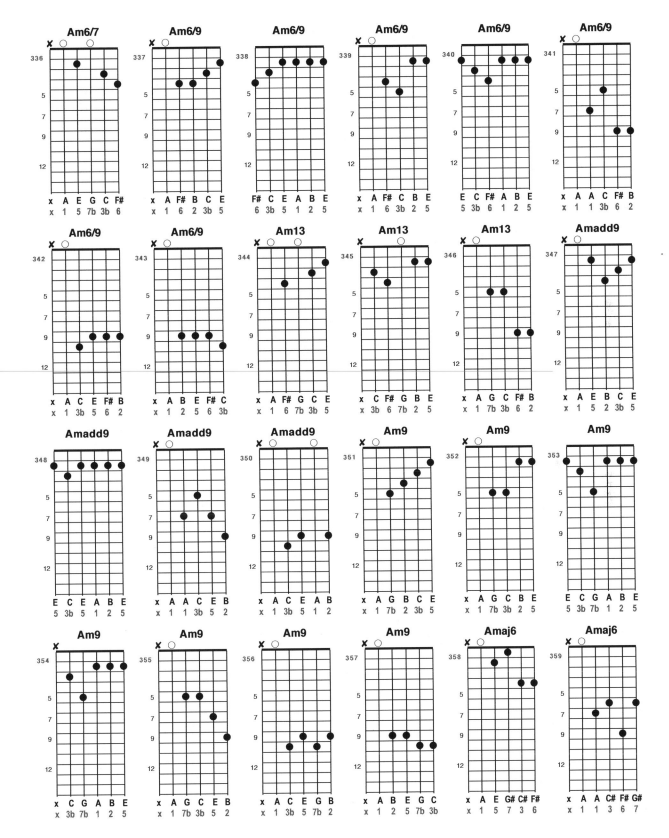

DADGAD Guitar Chords
TUNING: D A D G A D

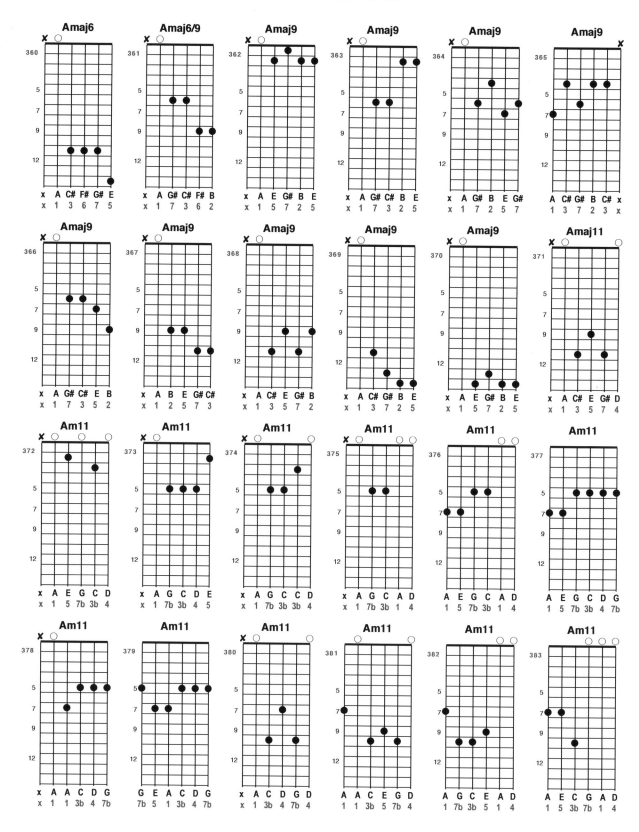

32

DADGAD Guitar Chords
TUNING: D A D G A D

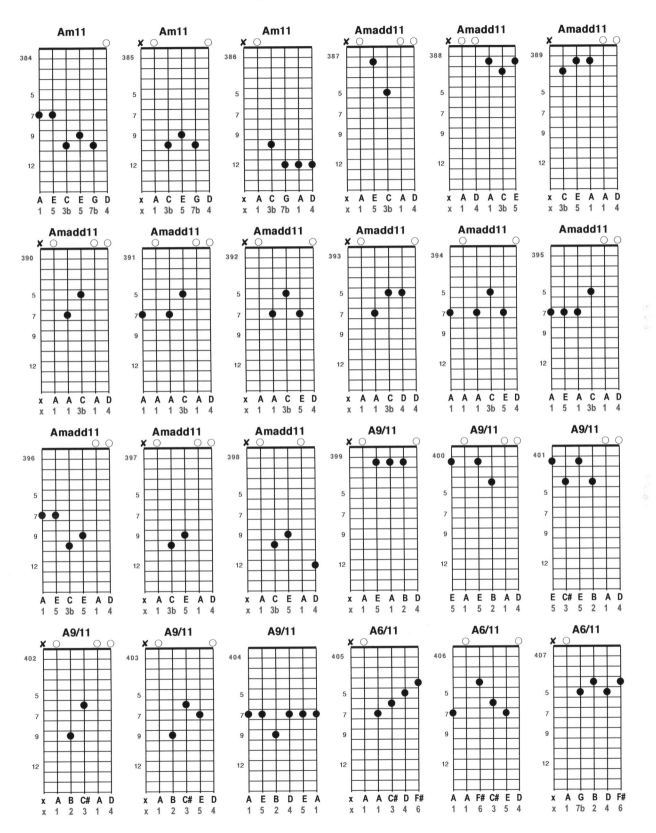

DADGAD Guitar Chords
TUNING: D A D G A D

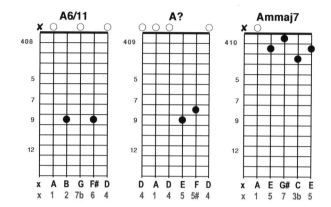

34

DADGAD Guitar Chords
TUNING: D A D G A D

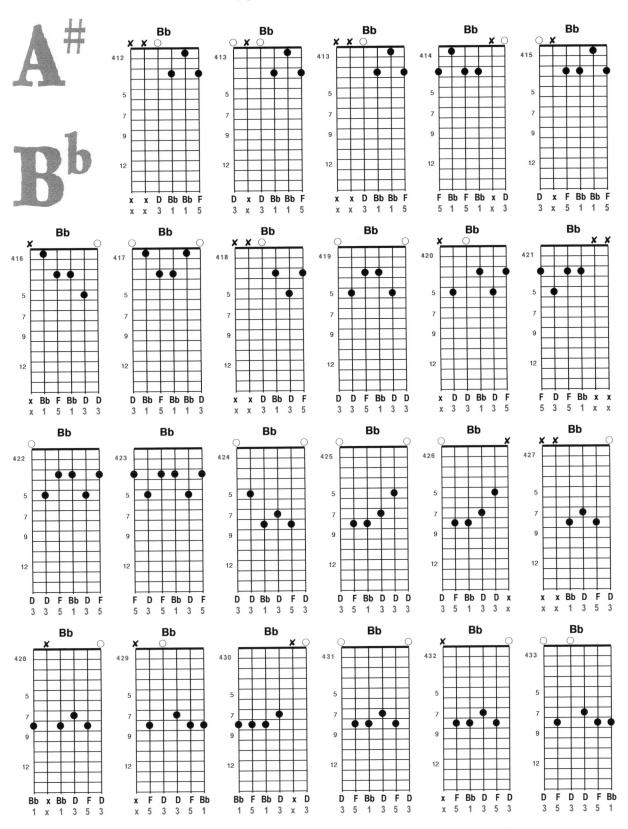

35

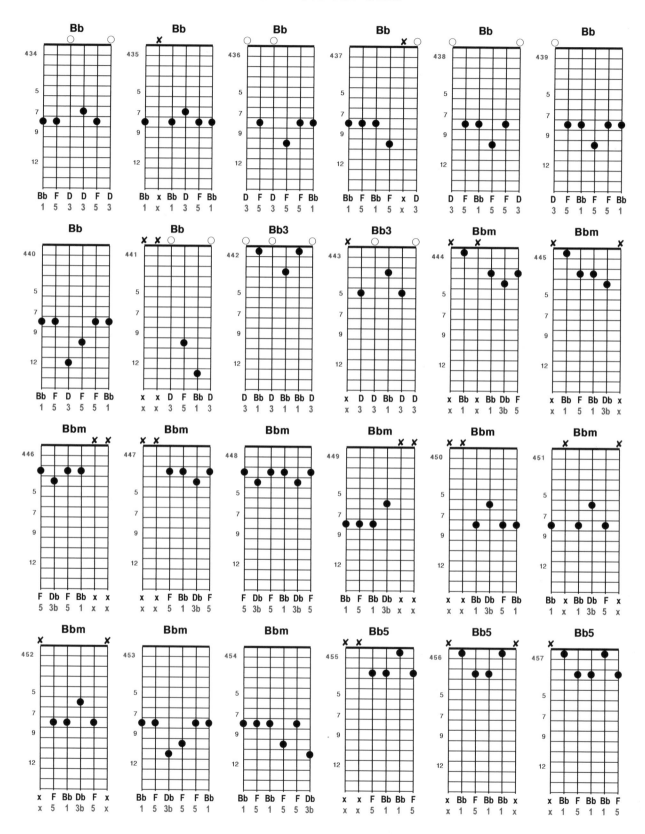

DADGAD Guitar Chords
TUNING: D A D G A D

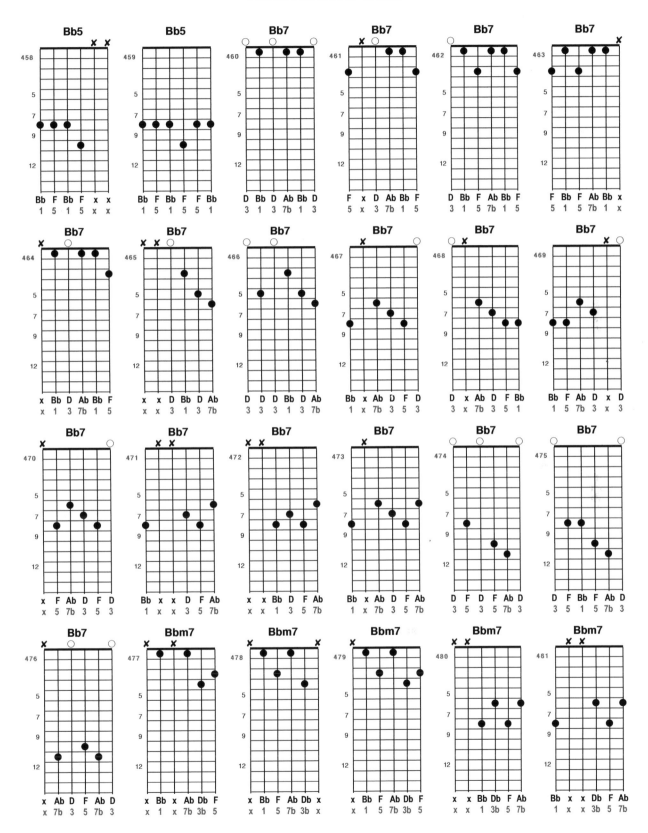

37

DADGAD Guitar Chords
TUNING: D A D G A D

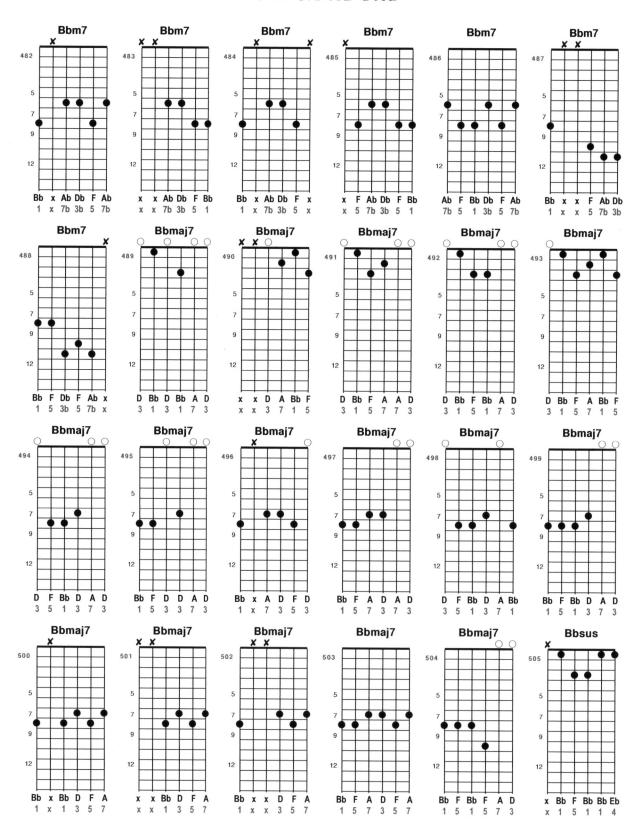

DADGAD Guitar Chords
TUNING: D A D G A D

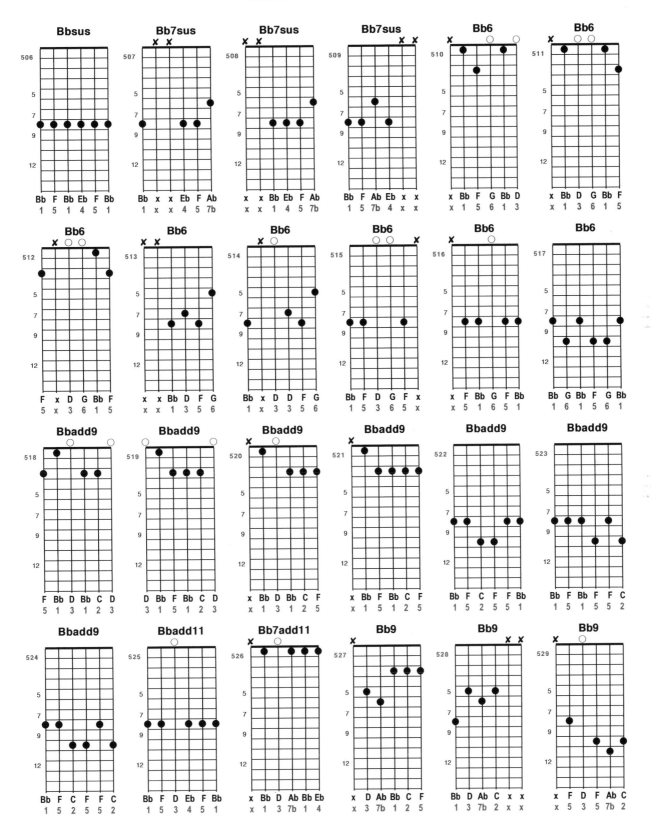

DADGAD Guitar Chords
TUNING: D A D G A D

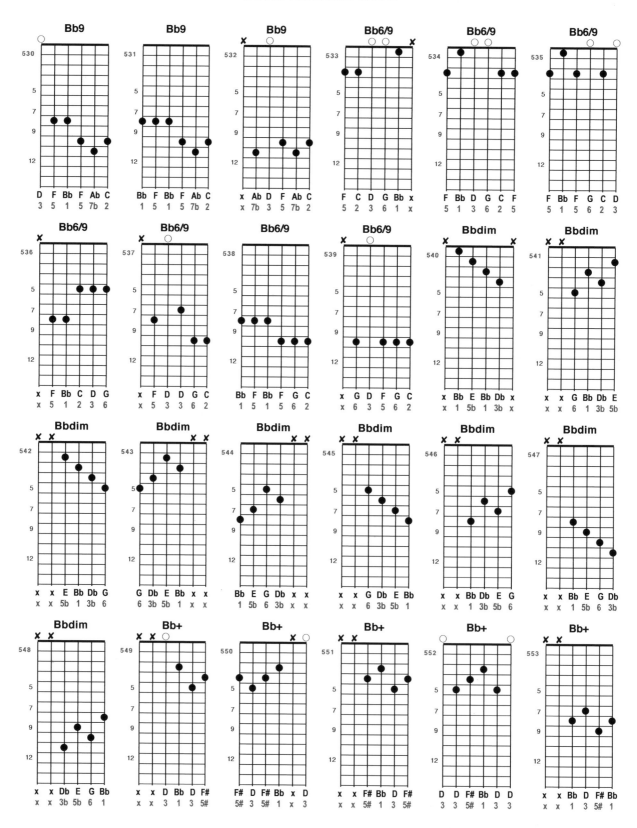

DADGAD Guitar Chords
TUNING: D A D G A D

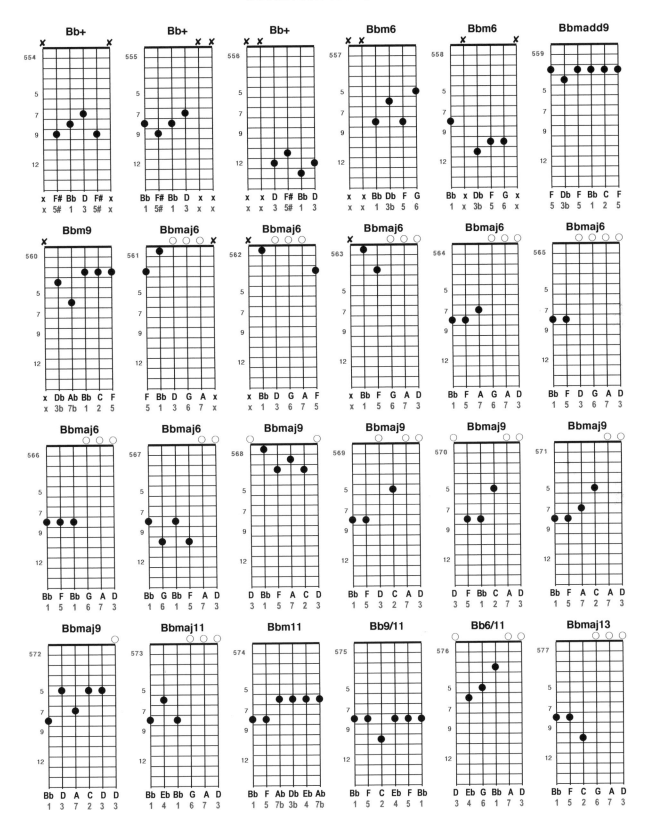

DADGAD Guitar Chords

TUNING: D A D G A D

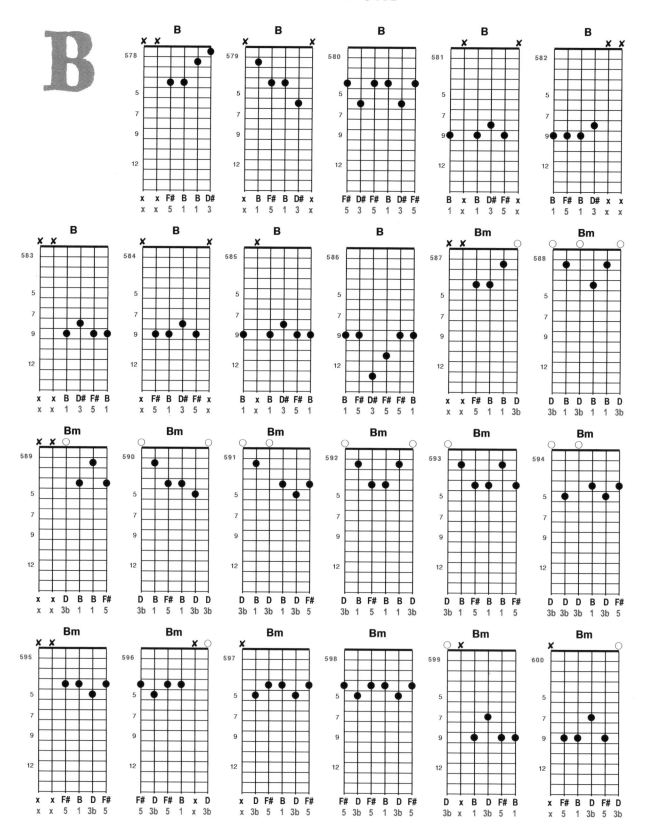

42

DADGAD Guitar Chords
TUNING: D A D G A D

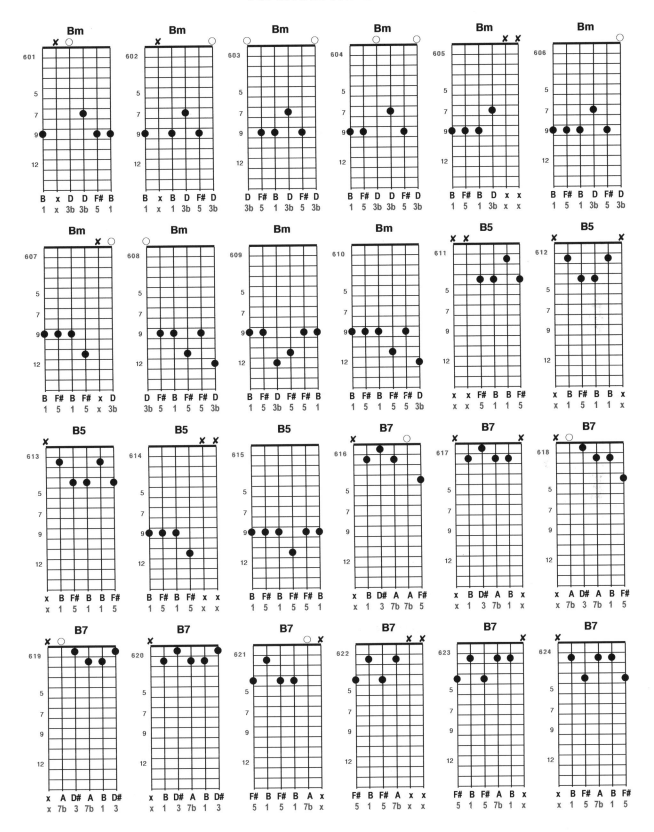

43

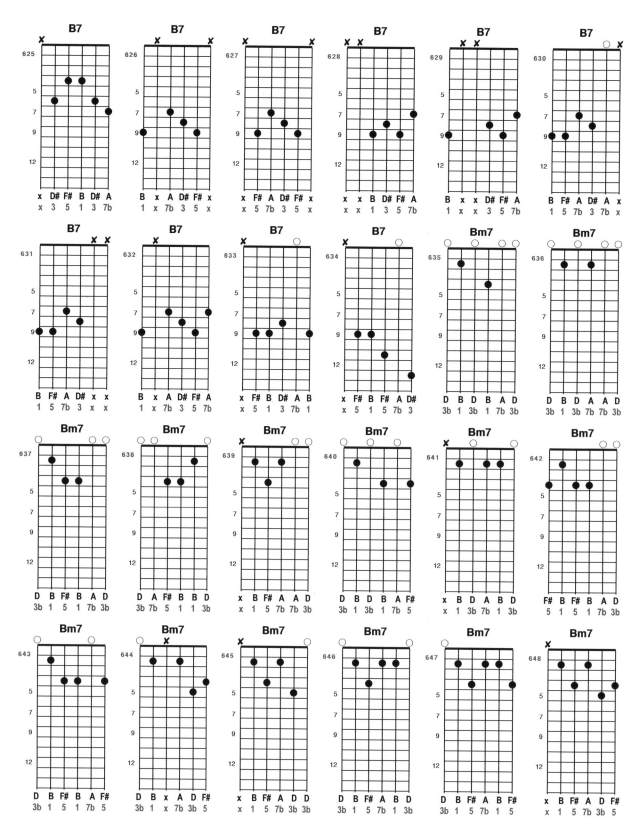

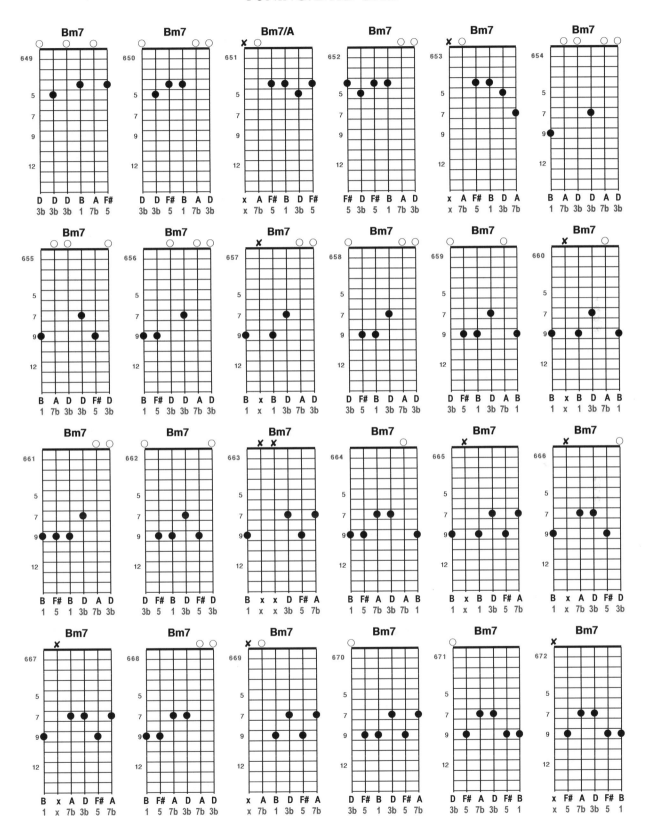

DADGAD Guitar Chords
TUNING: D A D G A D

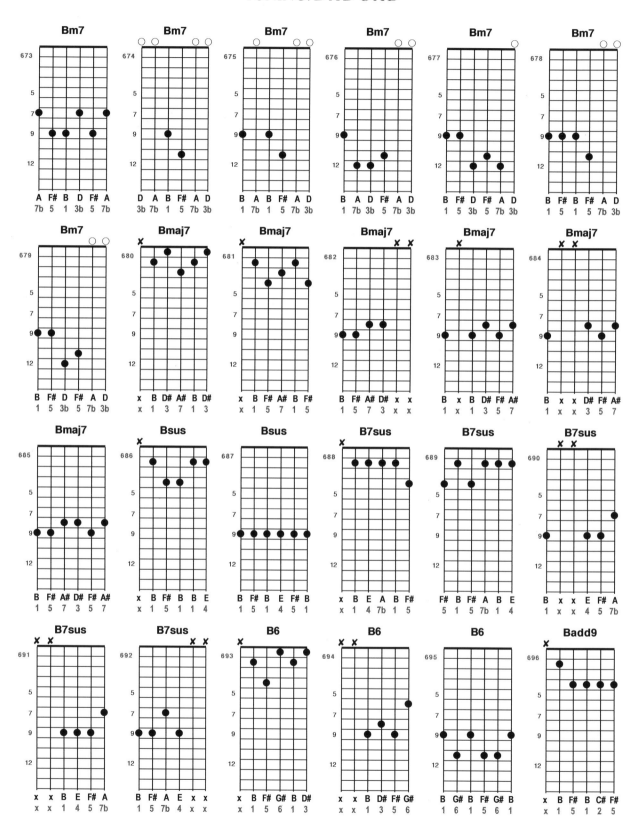

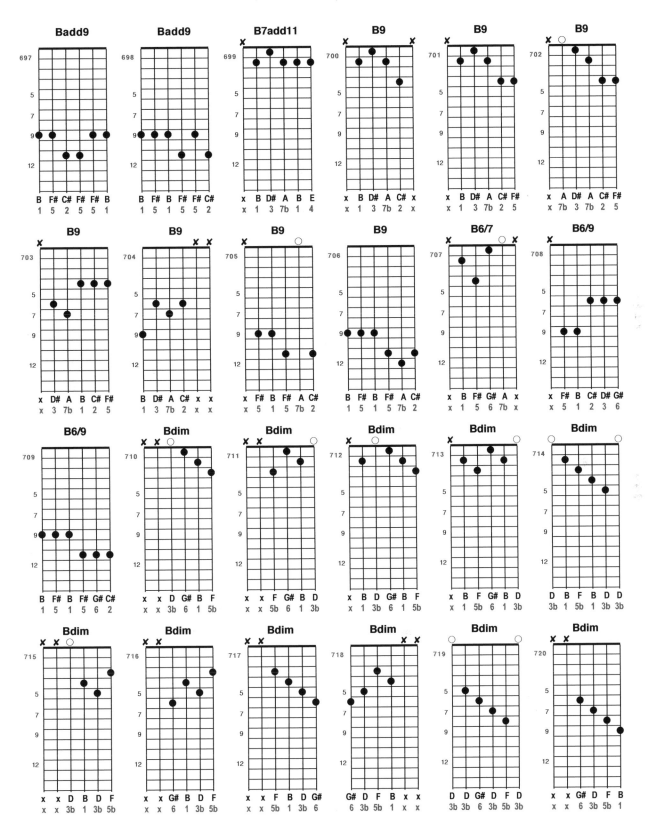

DADGAD Guitar Chords
TUNING: D A D G A D

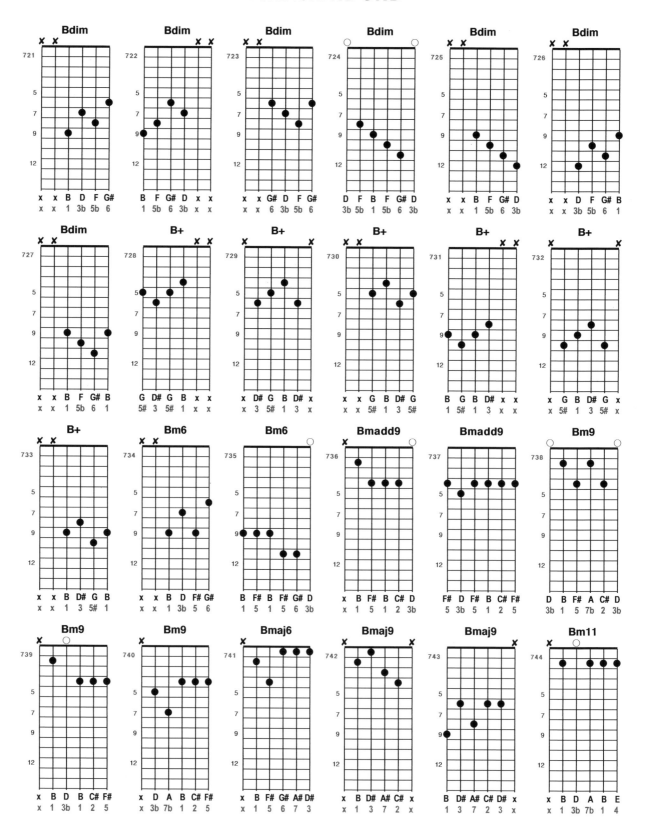

48

DADGAD Guitar Chords
TUNING: D A D G A D

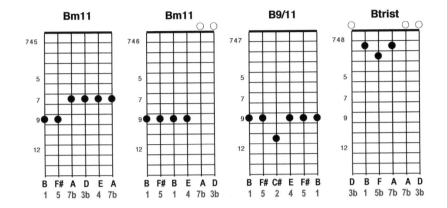

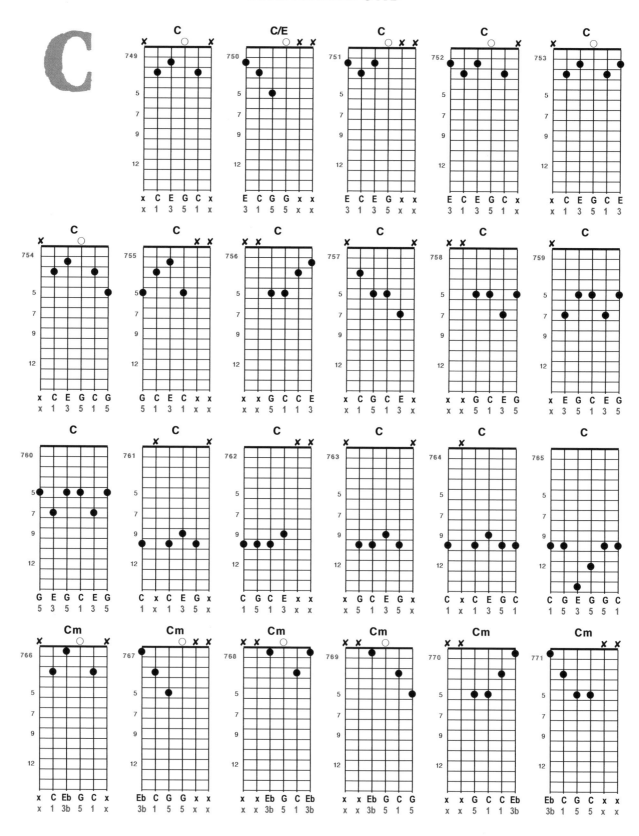

DADGAD Guitar Chords
TUNING: D A D G A D

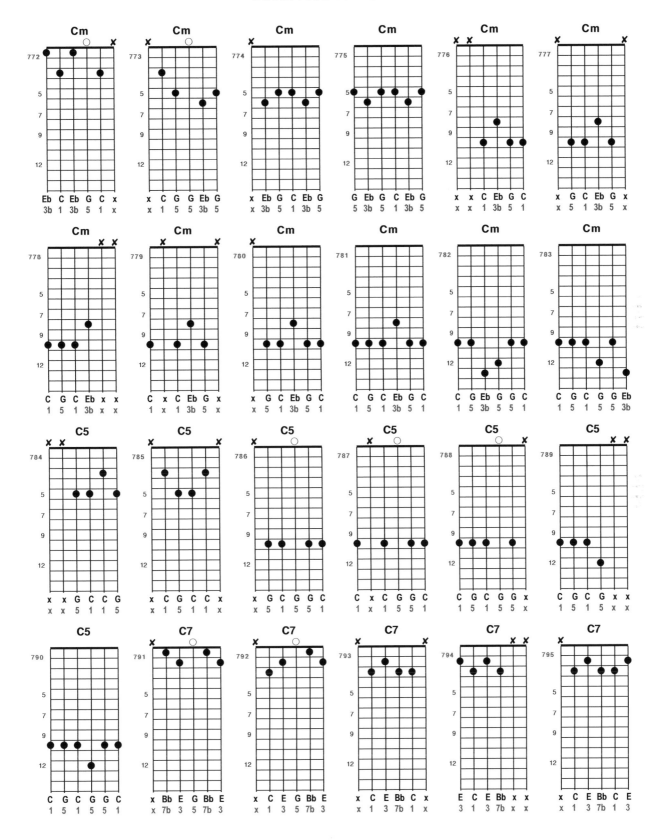

51

DADGAD Guitar Chords
TUNING: D A D G A D

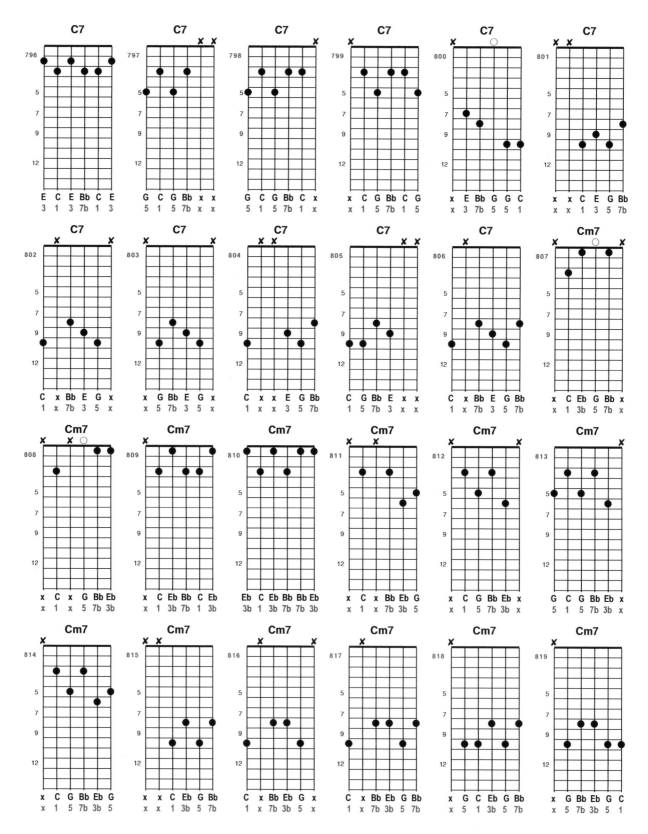

52

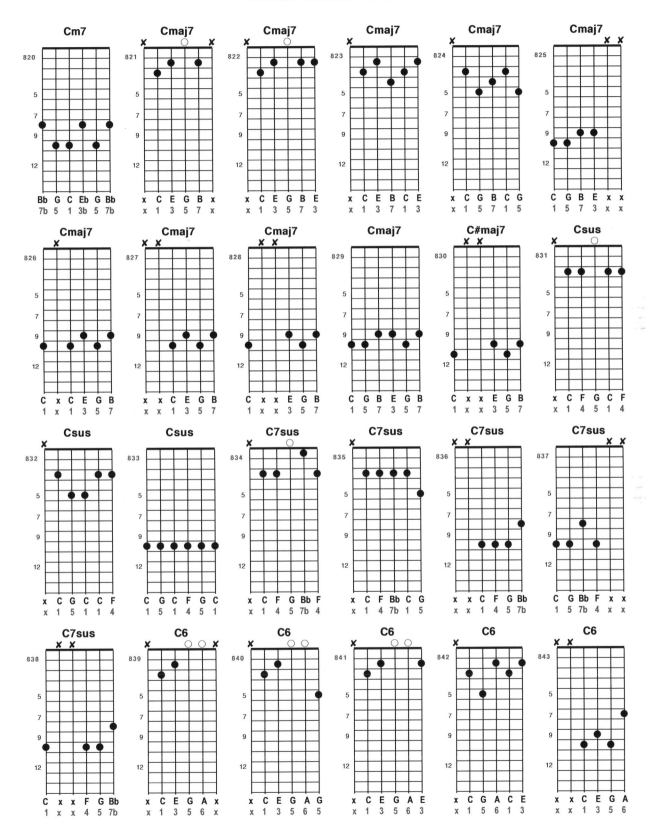

DADGAD Guitar Chords
TUNING: D A D G A D

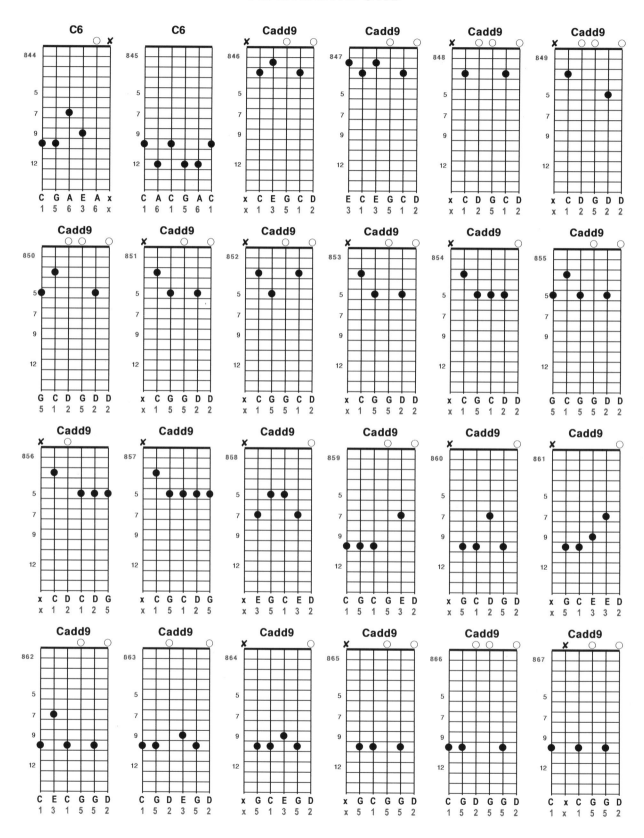

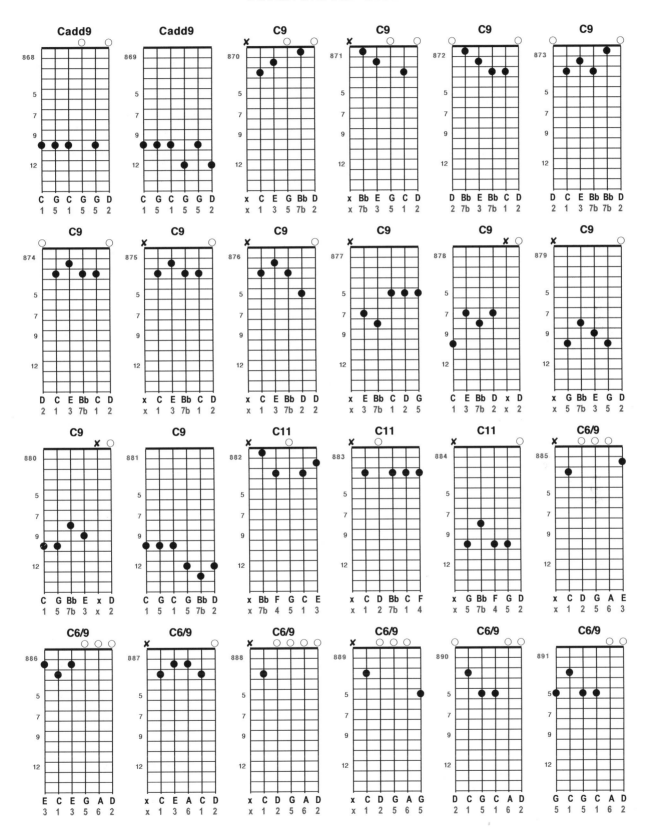

DADGAD Guitar Chords
TUNING: D A D G A D

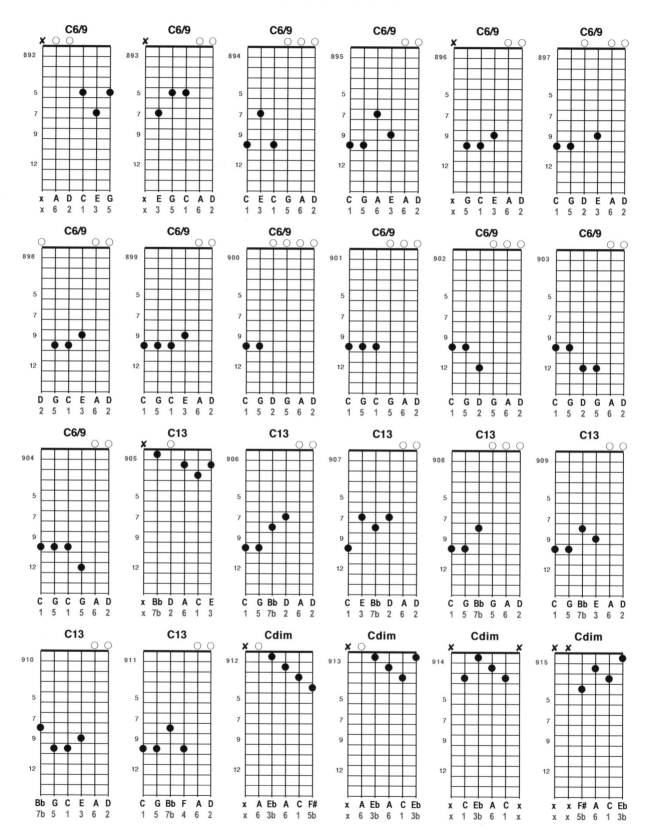

56

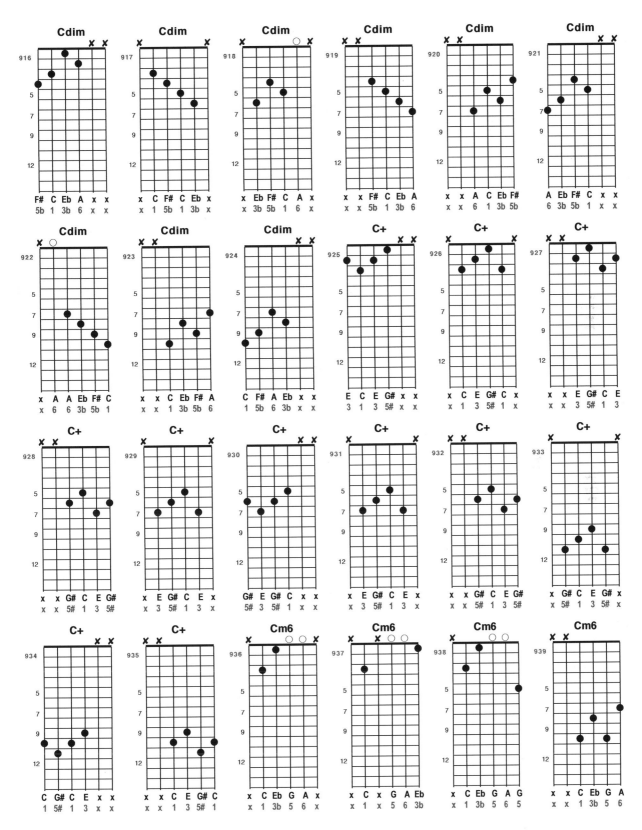

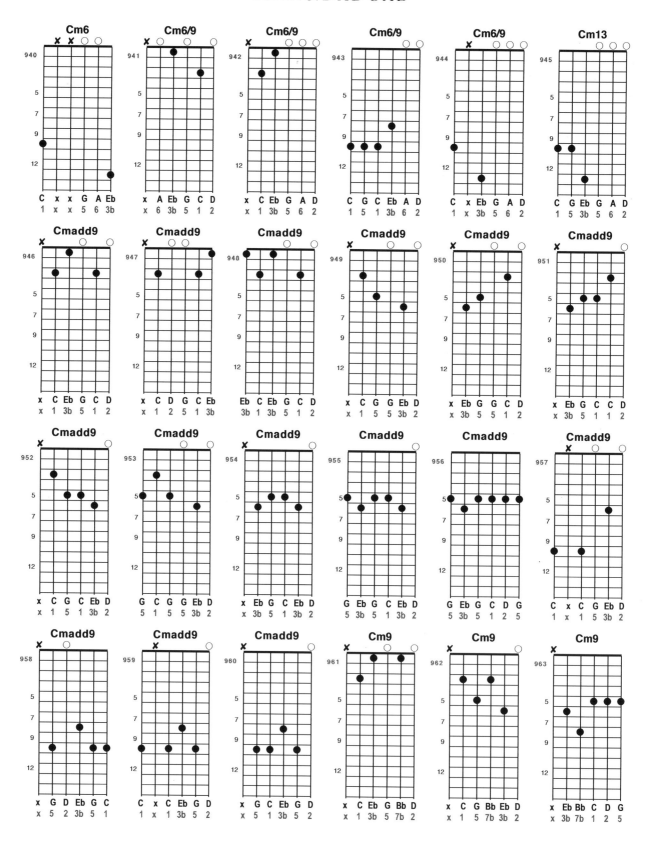

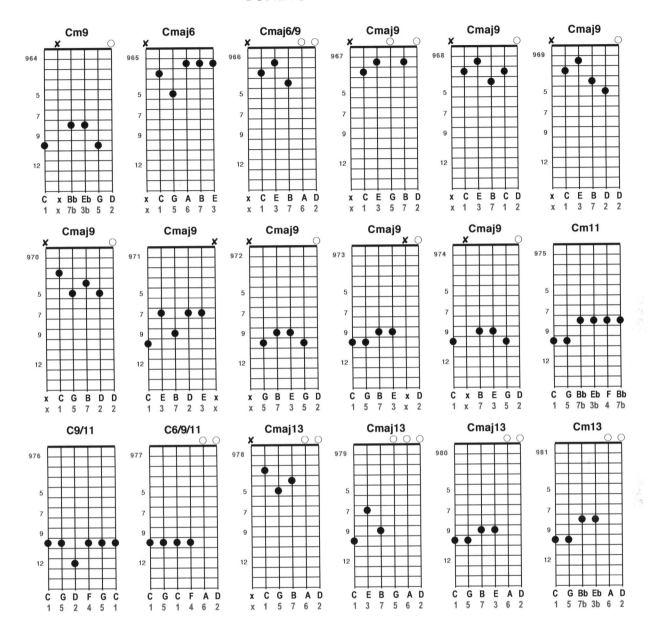

DADGAD Guitar Chords
TUNING: DADGAD

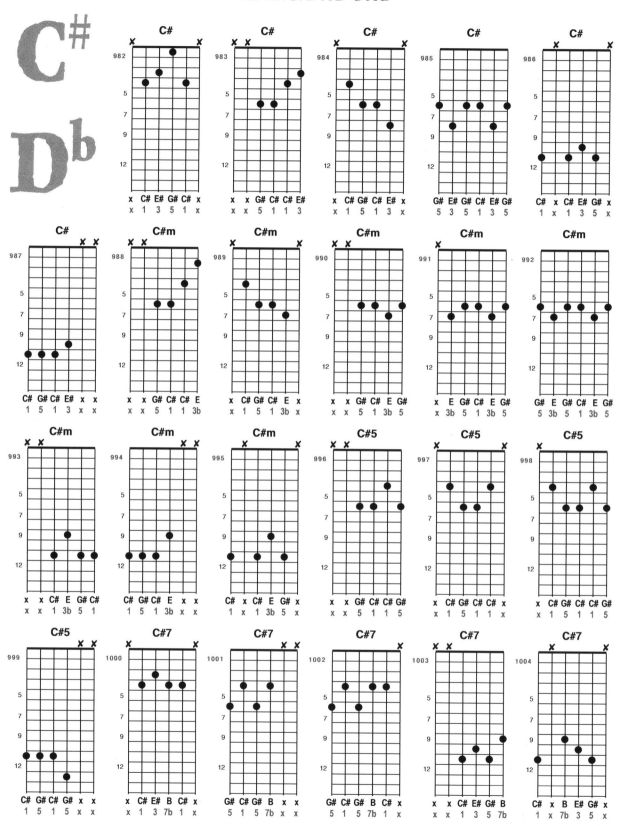

60

DADGAD Guitar Chords
TUNING: *D A D G A D*

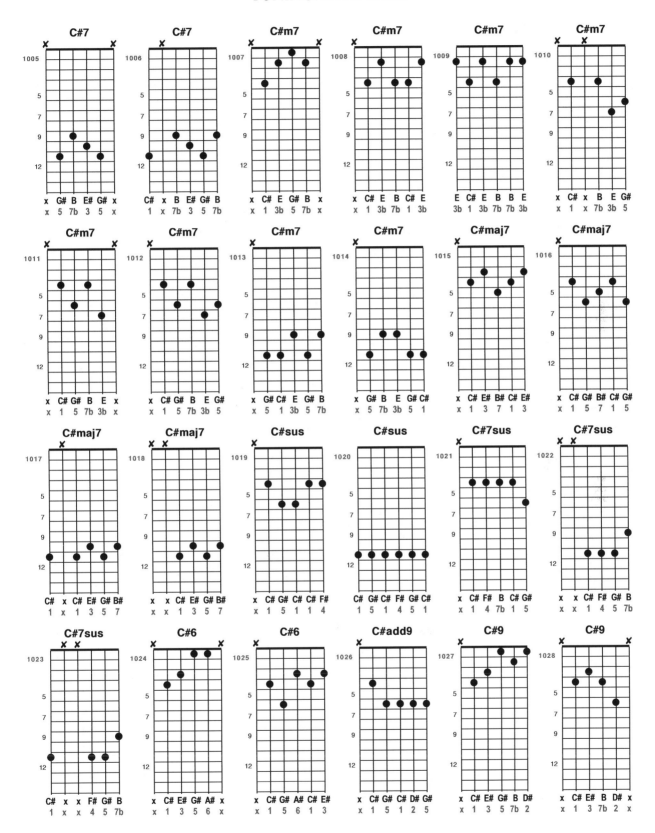

DADGAD Guitar Chords
TUNING: D A D G A D

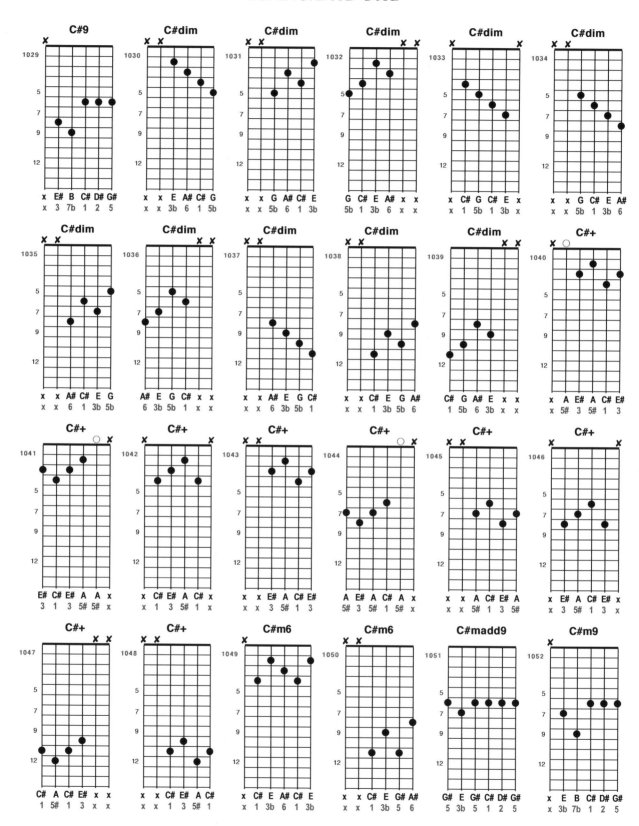

62

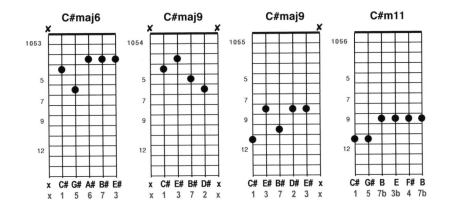

C#maj6	C#maj9	C#maj9	C#m11
x C# G# A# B# E#	x C# E# B# D# x	C# E# B# D# E# x	C# G# B E F# B
x 1 5 6 7 3	x 1 3 7 2 x	1 3 7 2 3 x	1 5 7b 3b 4 7b

DADGAD Guitar Chords
TUNING: D A D G A D

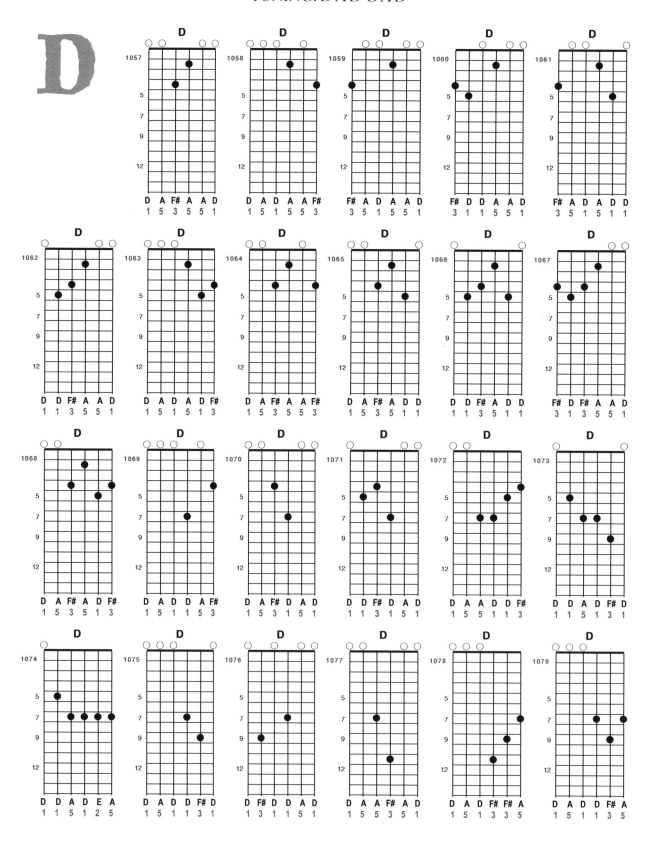

64

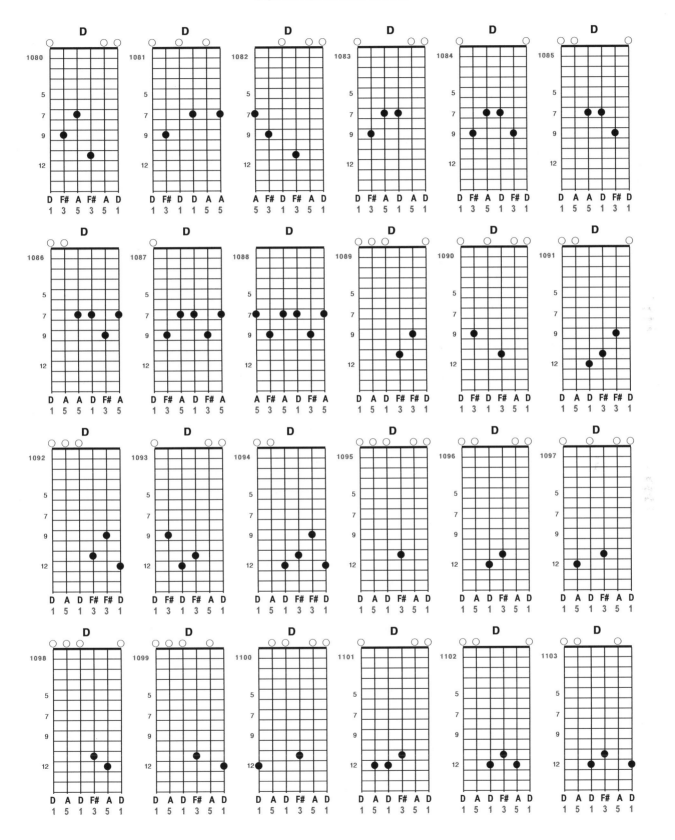

DADGAD Guitar Chords
TUNING: D A D G A D

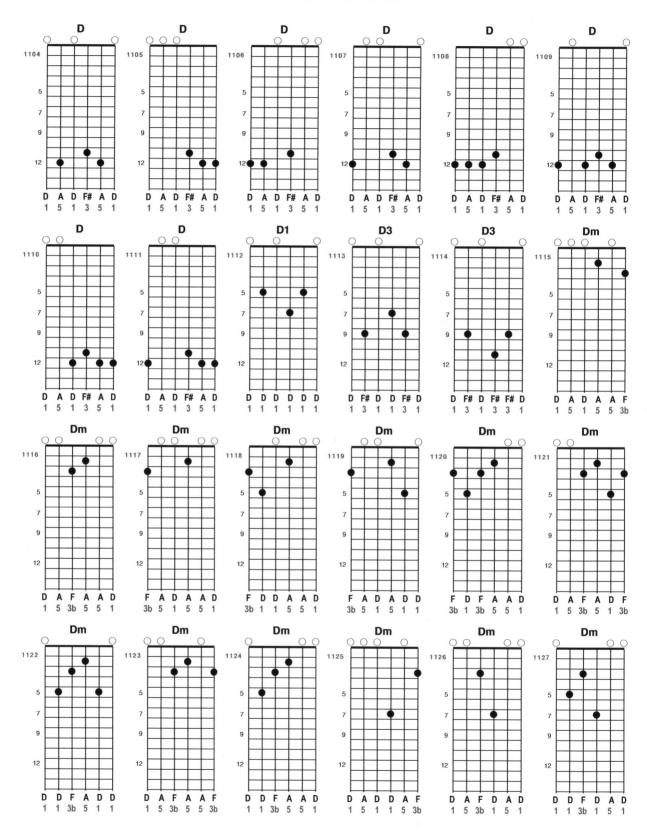

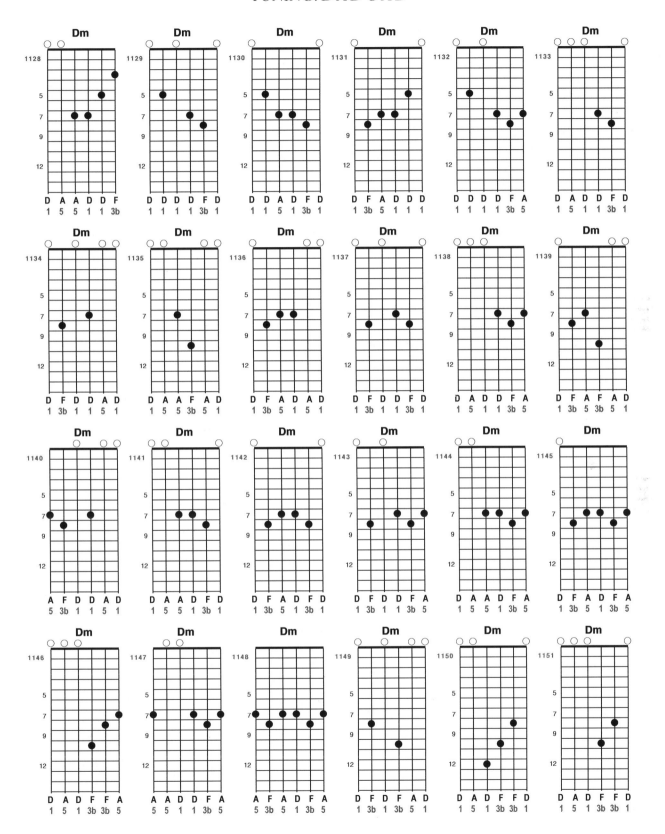

TUNING: D A D G A D

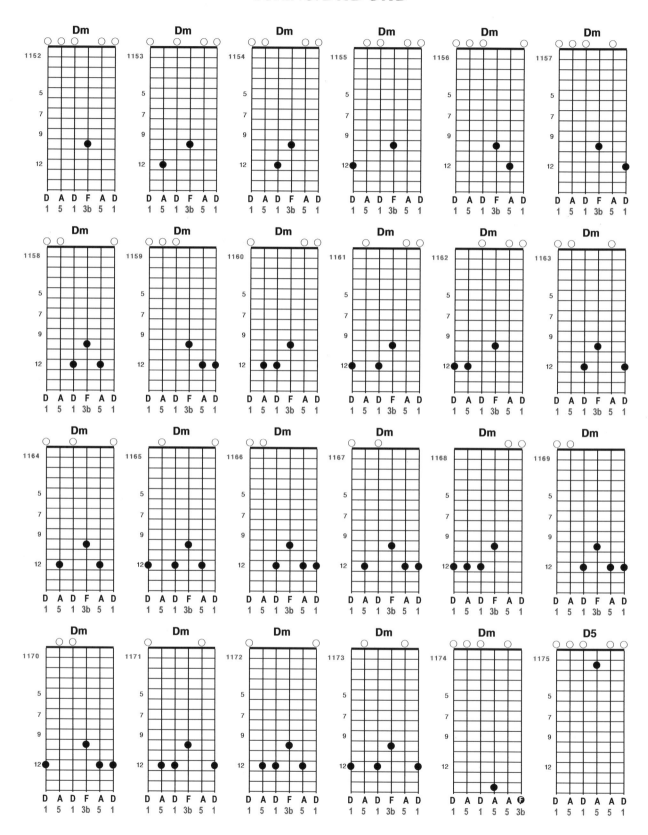

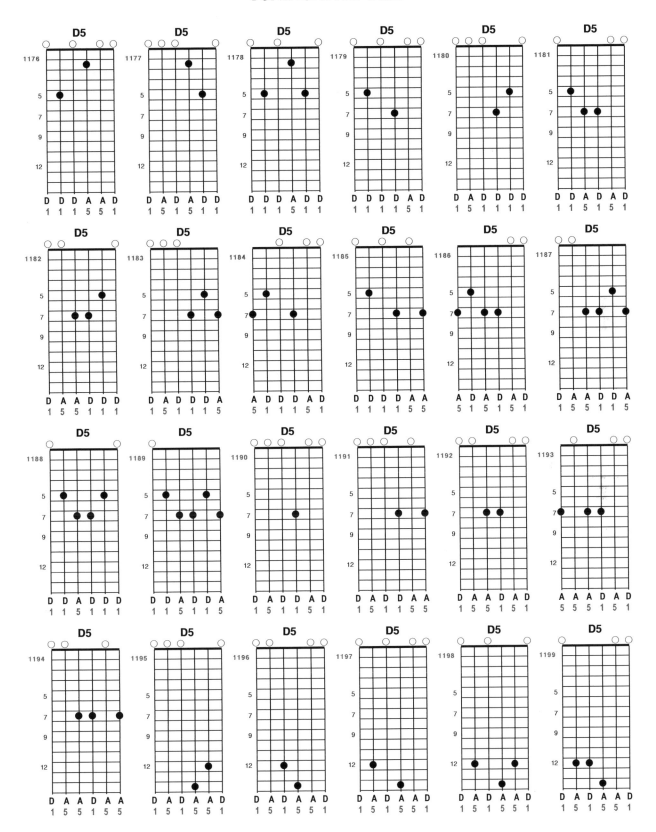

69

DADGAD Guitar Chords
TUNING: D A D G A D

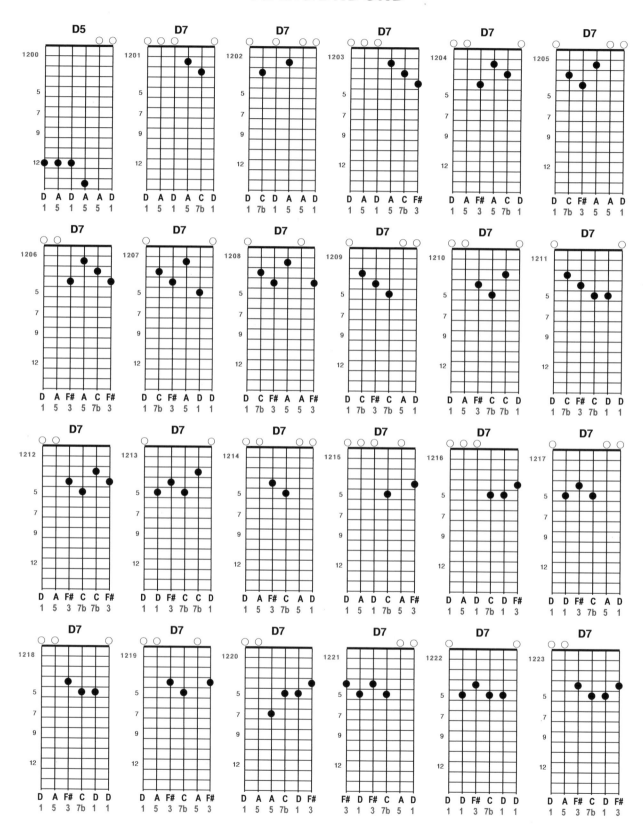

70

DADGAD Guitar Chords

TUNING: D A D G A D

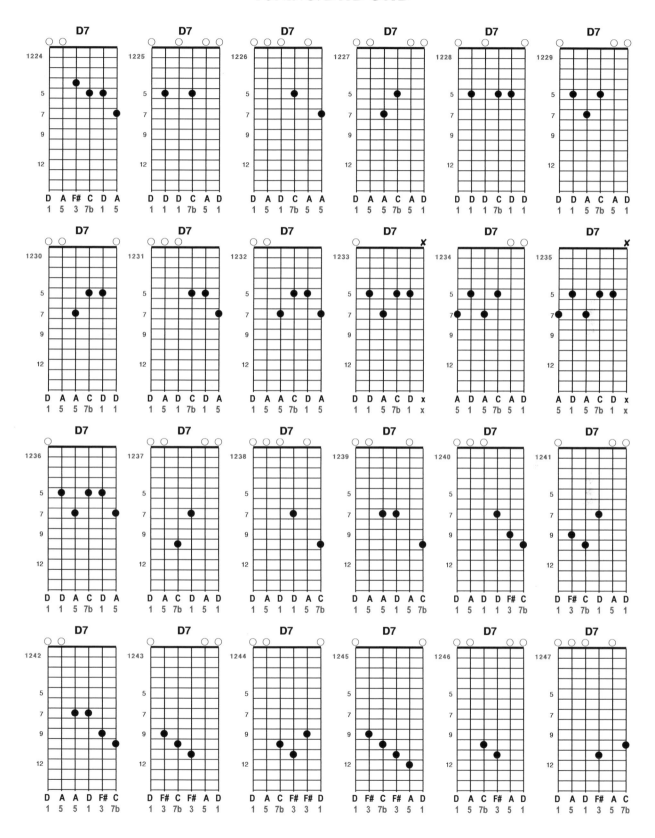

DADGAD Guitar Chords
TUNING: D A D G A D

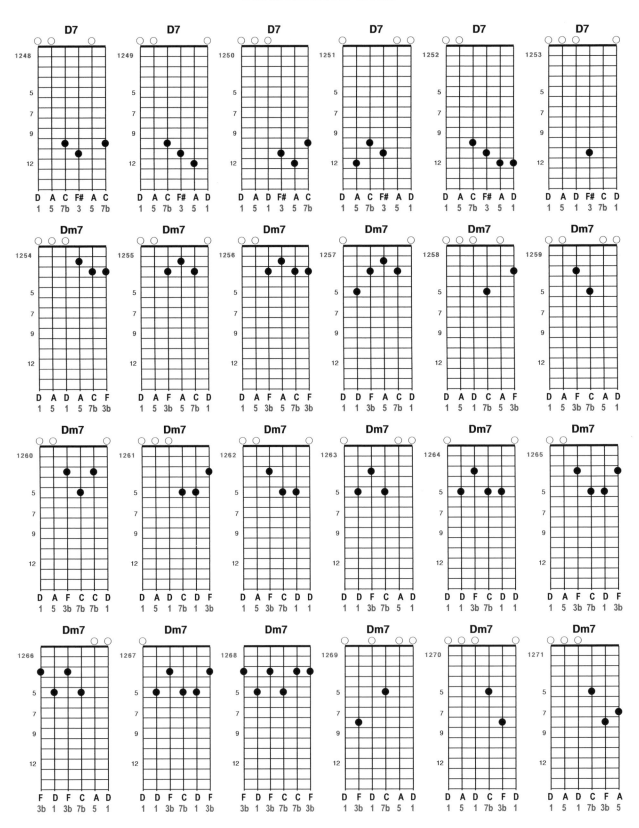

DADGAD Guitar Chords
TUNING: D A D G A D

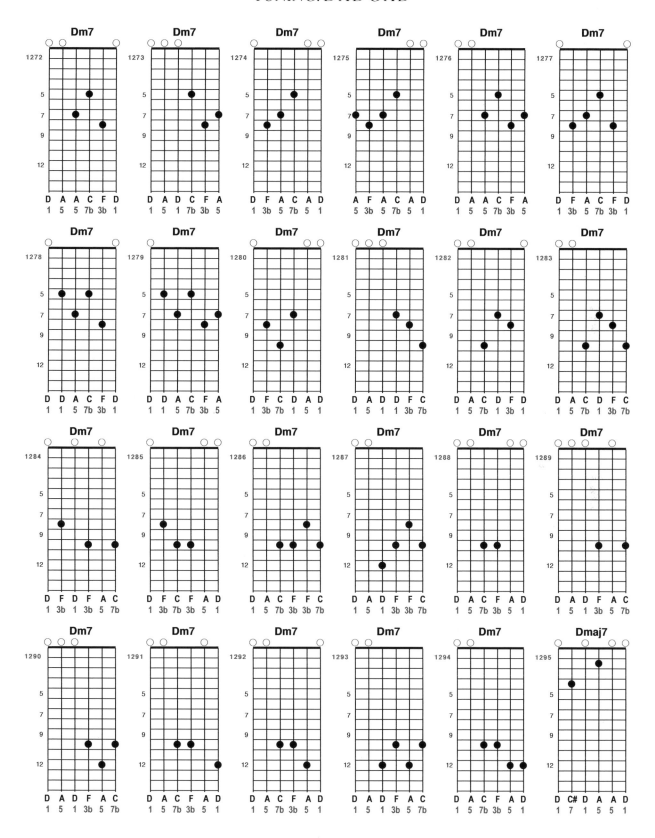

DADGAD Guitar Chords

TUNING: D A D G A D

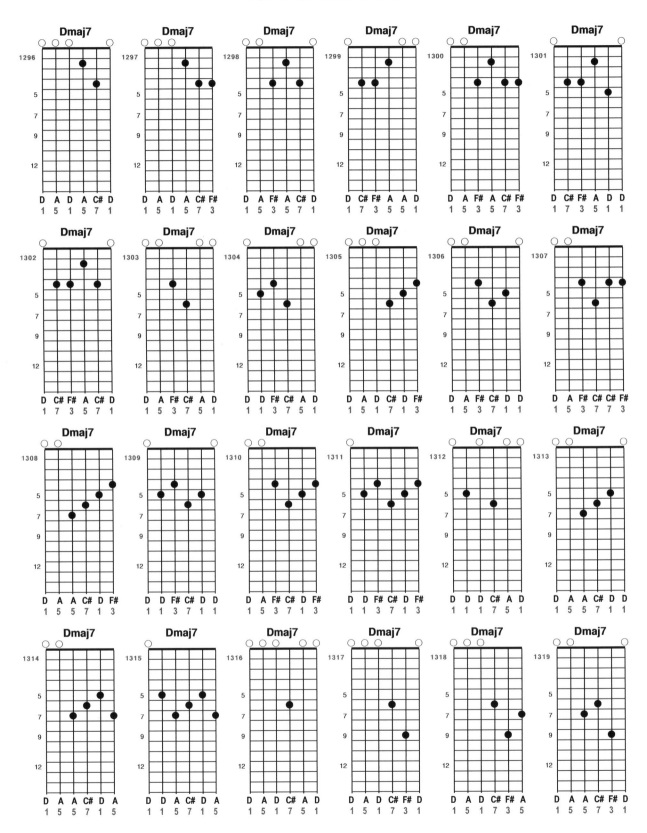

74

DADGAD Guitar Chords
TUNING: D A D G A D

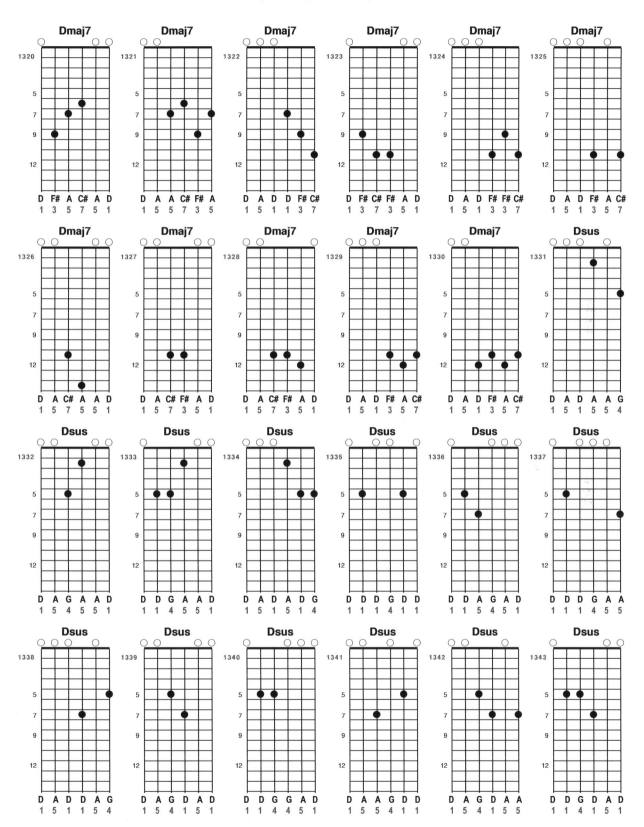

DADGAD Guitar Chords
TUNING: D A D G A D

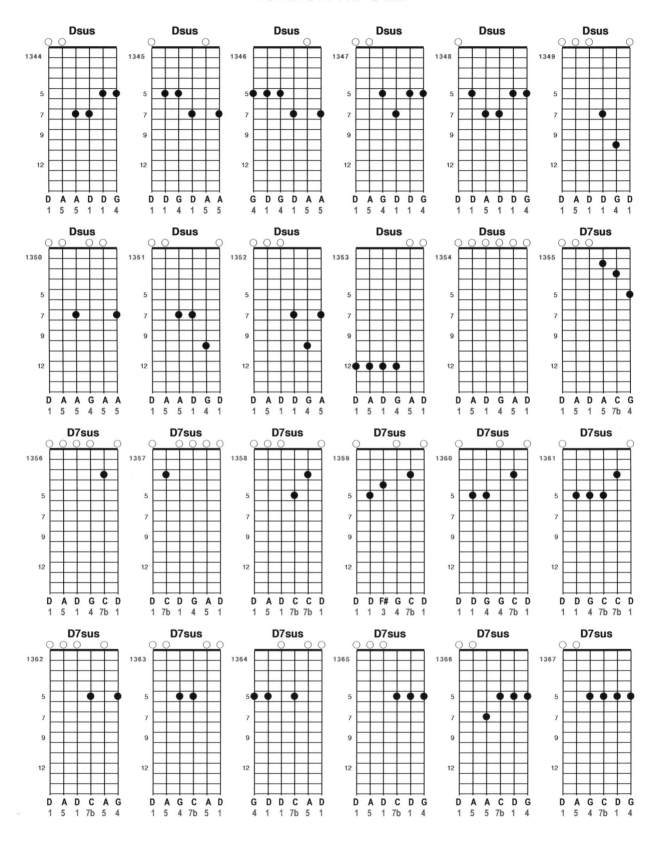

76

DADGAD Guitar Chords
TUNING: D A D G A D

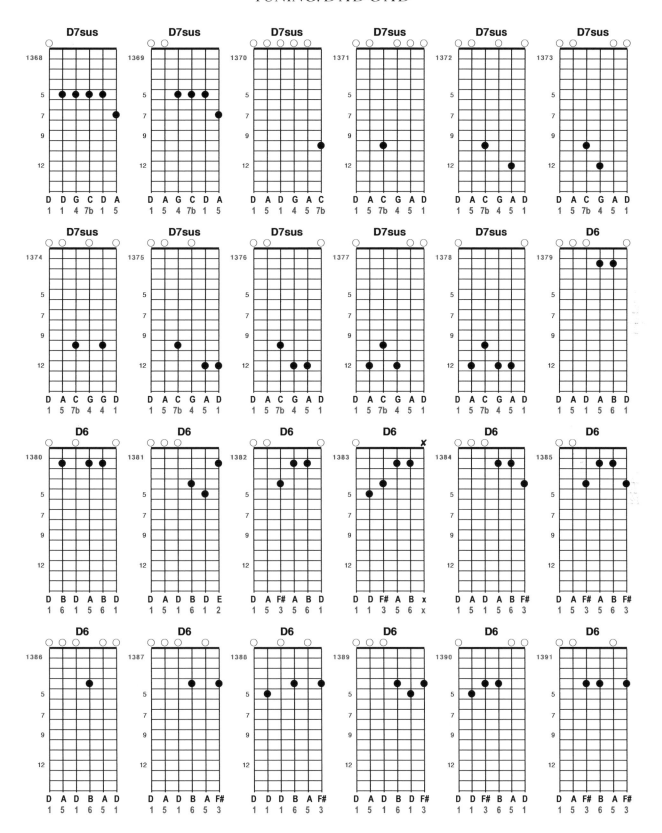

TUNING: D A D G A D

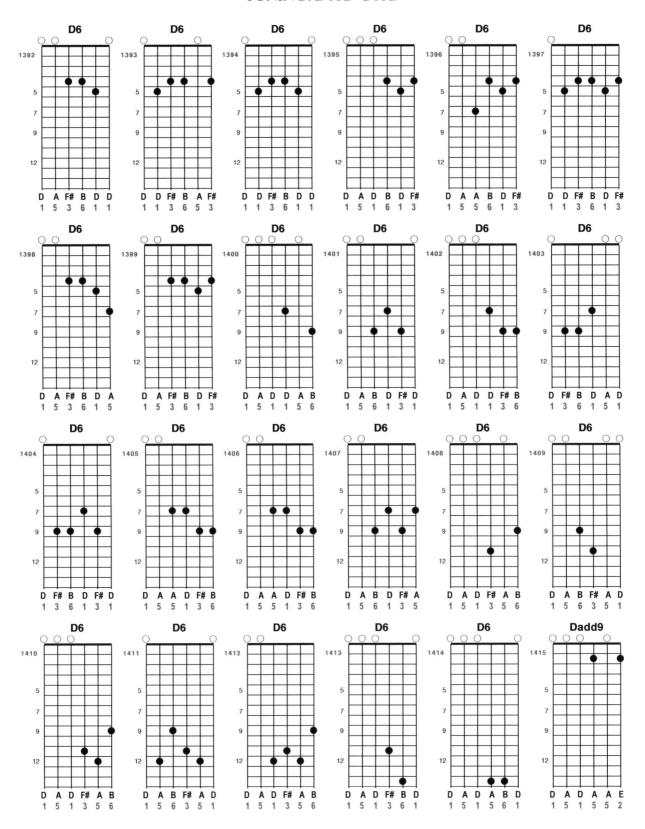

DADGAD Guitar Chords
TUNING: D A D G A D

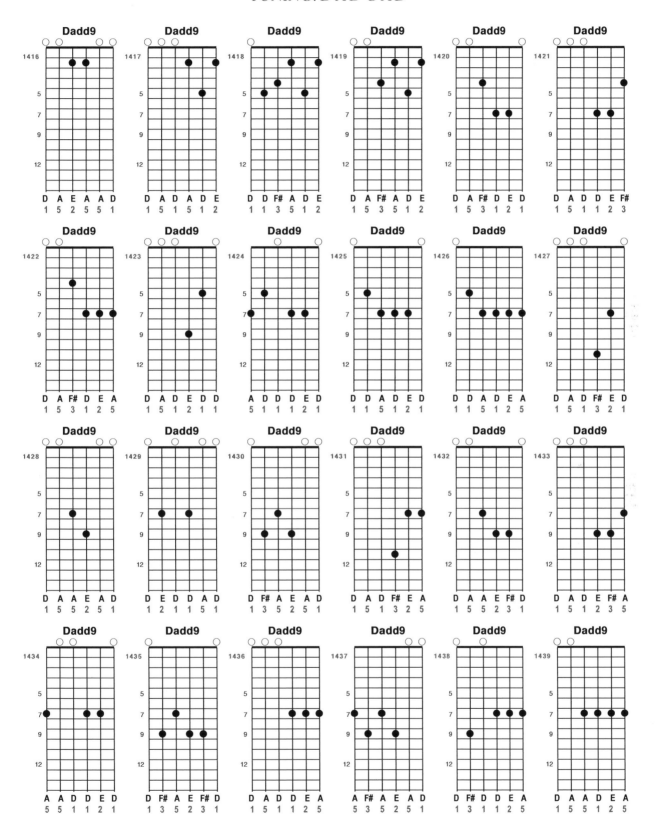

DADGAD Guitar Chords
TUNING: D A D G A D

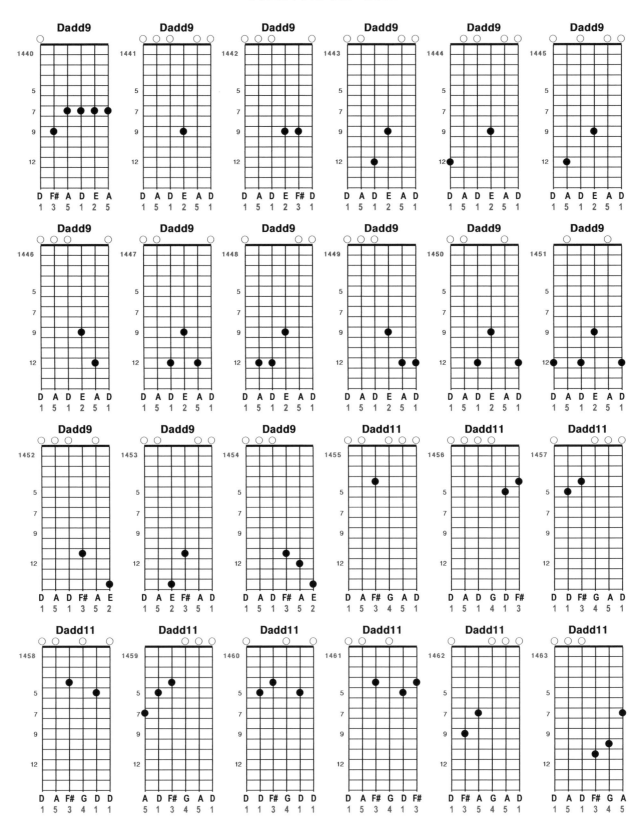

DADGAD Guitar Chords
TUNING: D A D G A D

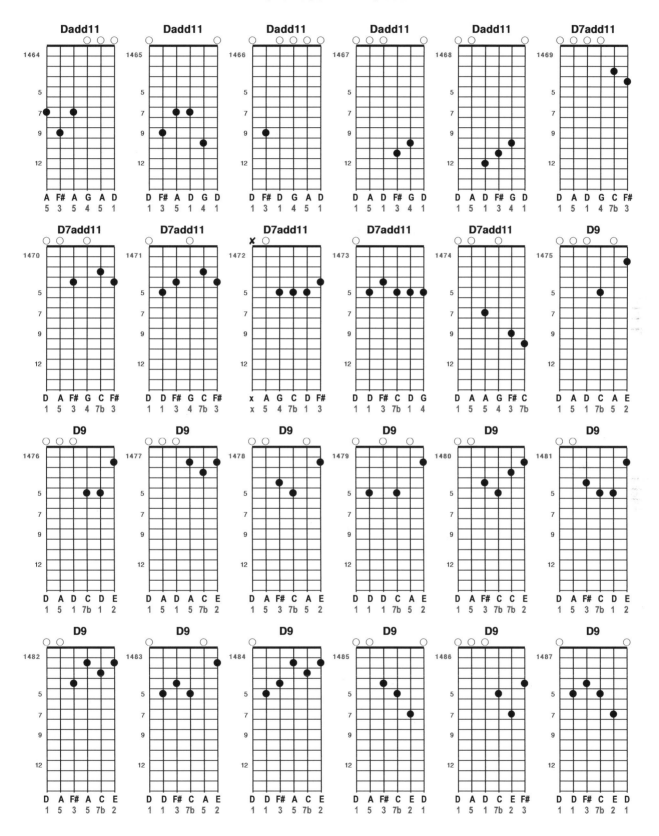

DADGAD Guitar Chords
TUNING: D A D G A D

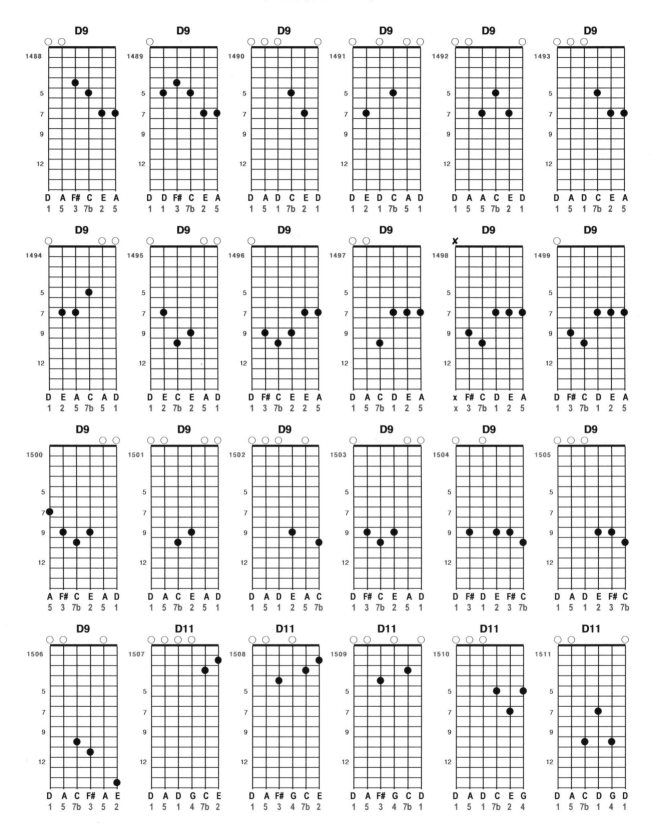

82

DADGAD Guitar Chords
TUNING: D A D G A D

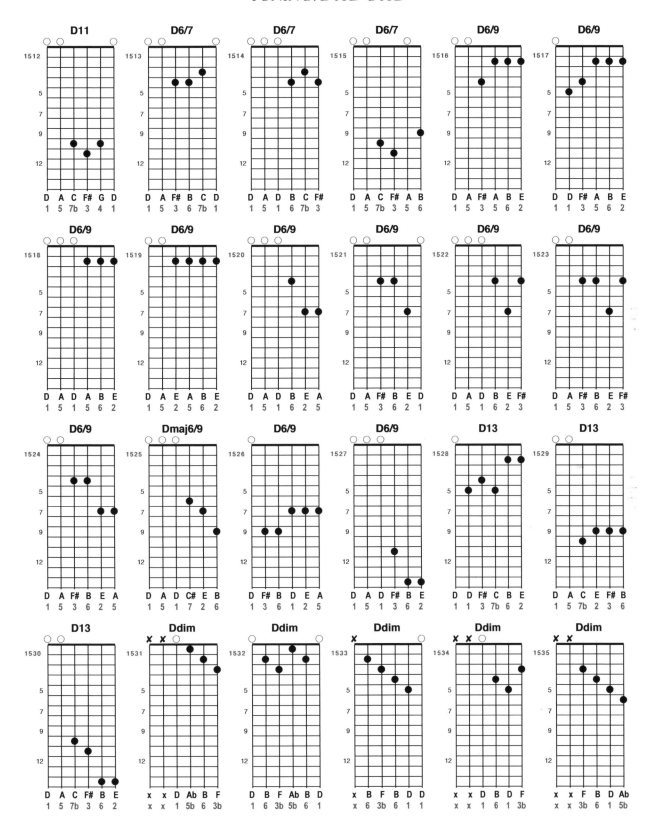

83

DADGAD Guitar Chords
TUNING: D A D G A D

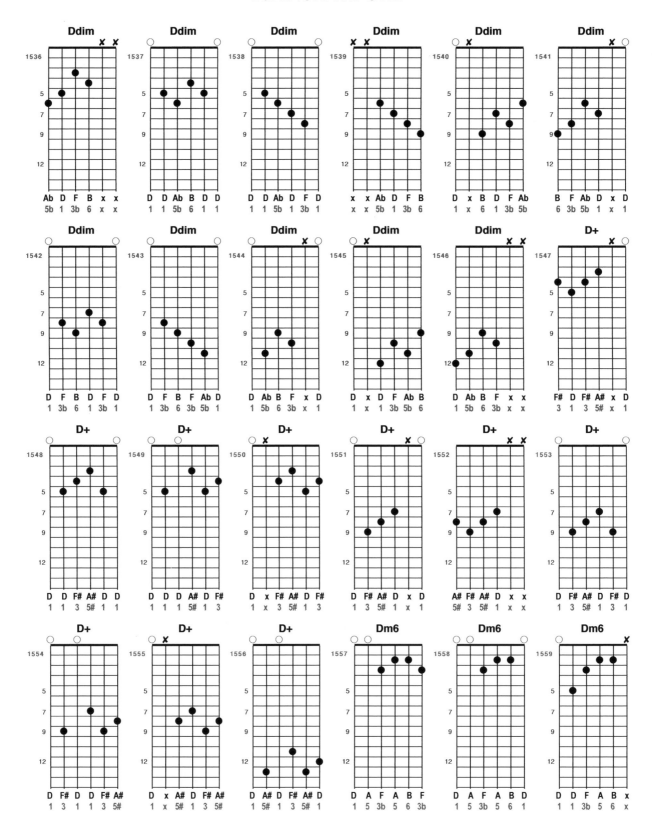

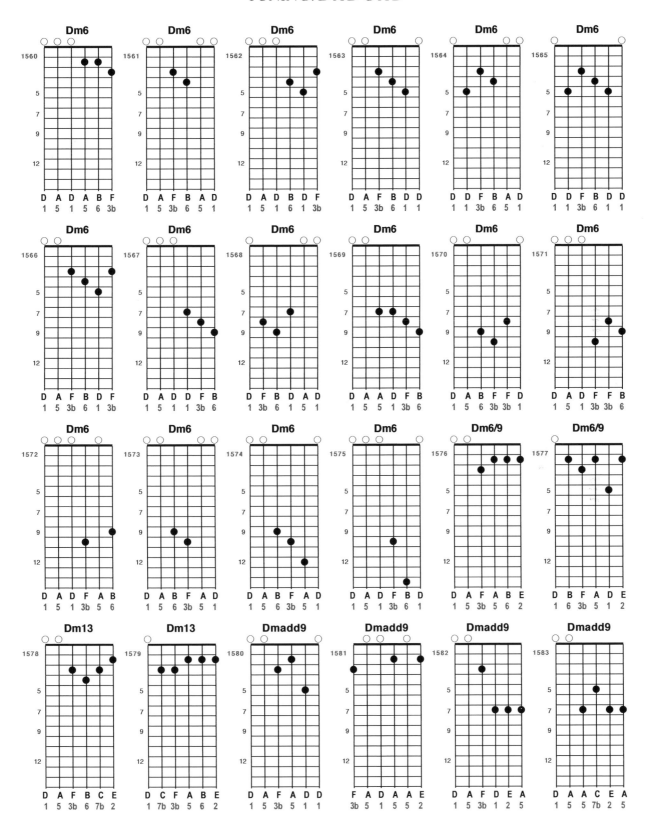

DADGAD Guitar Chords
TUNING: D A D G A D

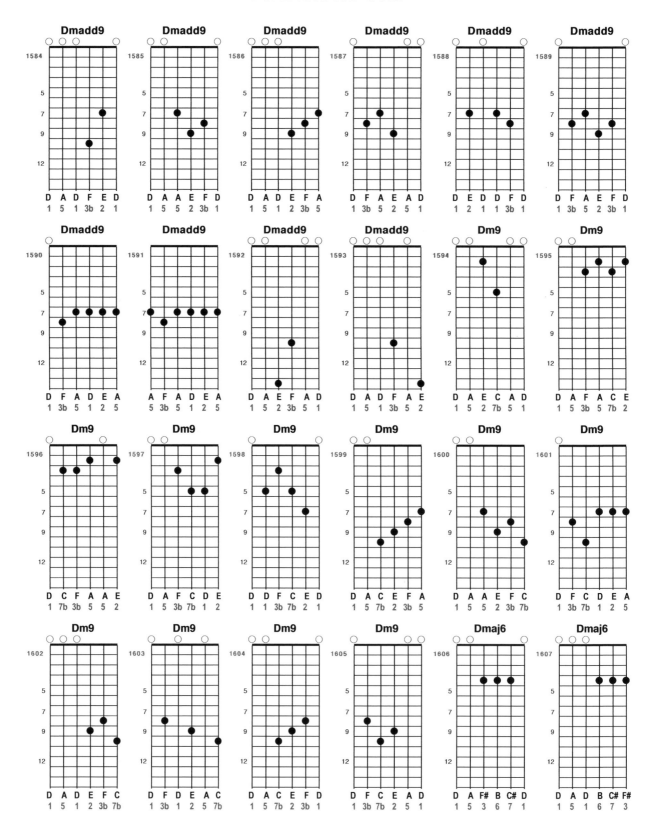

86

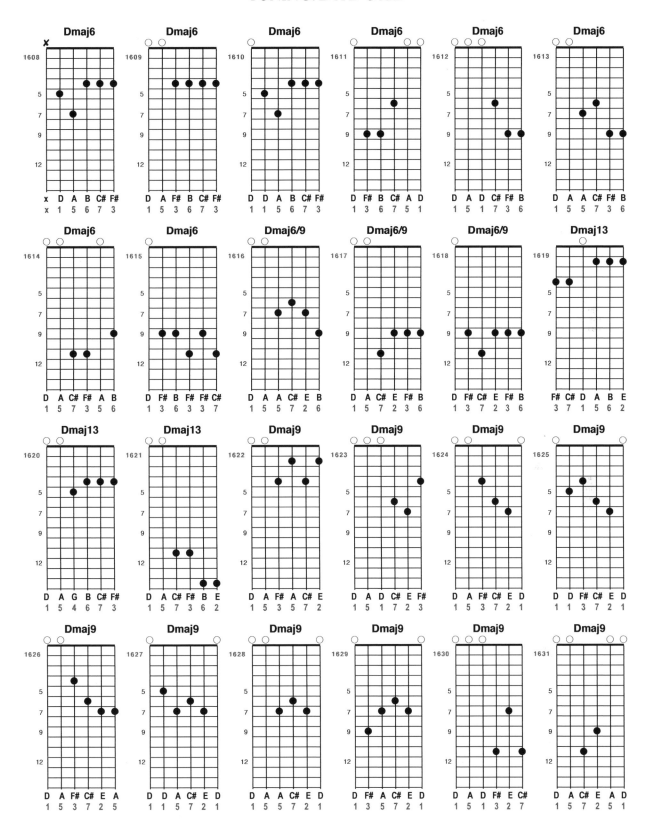

DADGAD Guitar Chords
TUNING: D A D G A D

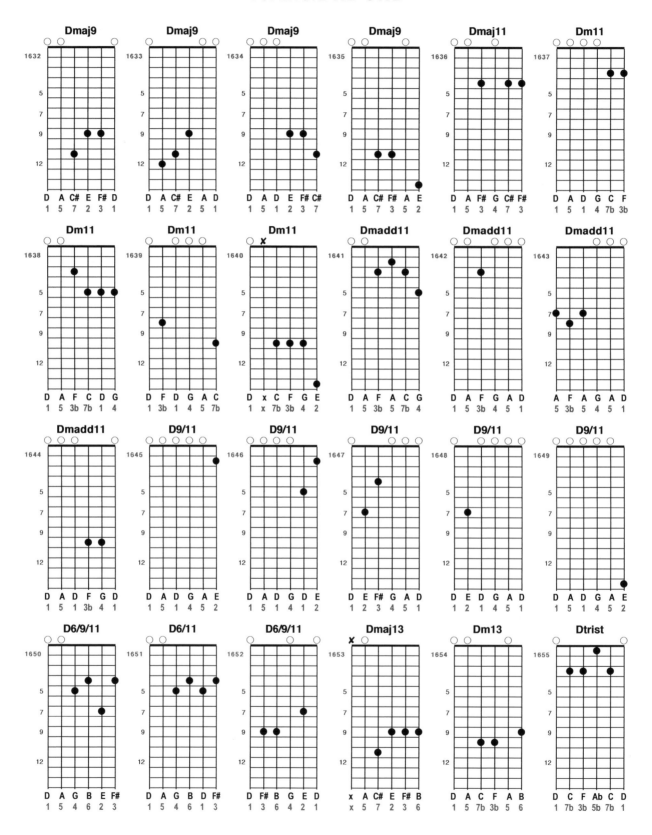

DADGAD Guitar Chords
TUNING: D A D G A D

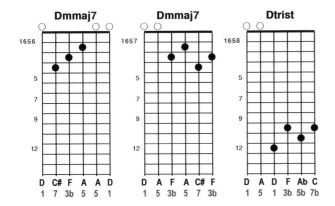

Dmmaj7	Dmmaj7	Dtrist
1656	1657	1658
D C# F A A D	D A F A C# F	D A D F Ab C
1 7 3b 5 5 1	1 5 3b 5 7 3b	1 5 1 3b 5b 7b

89

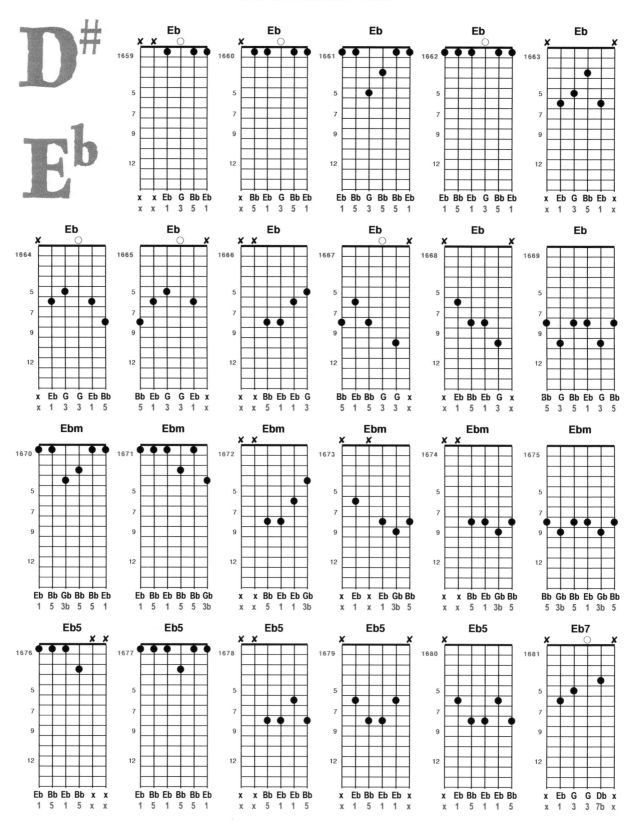

DADGAD Guitar Chords
TUNING: D A D G A D

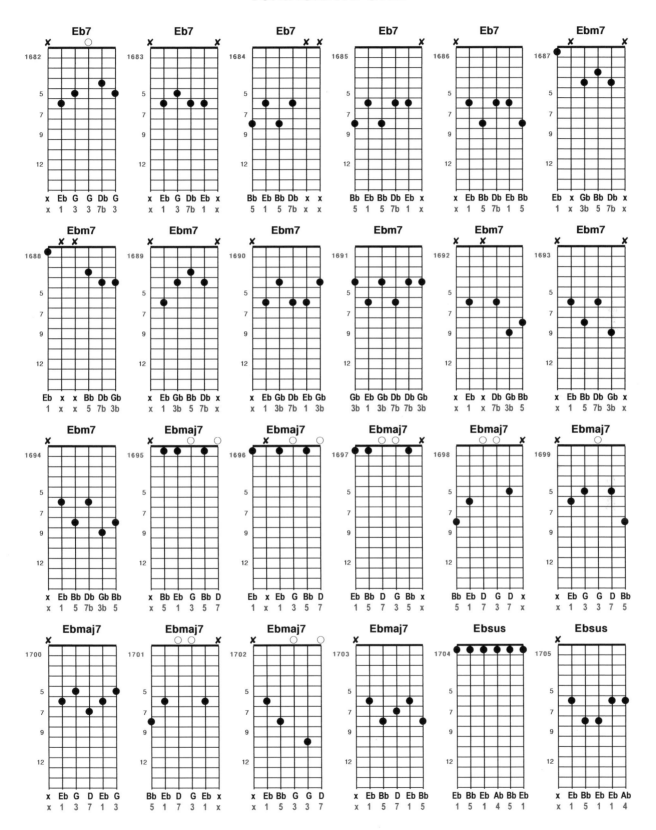

91

DADGAD Guitar Chords
TUNING: D A D G A D

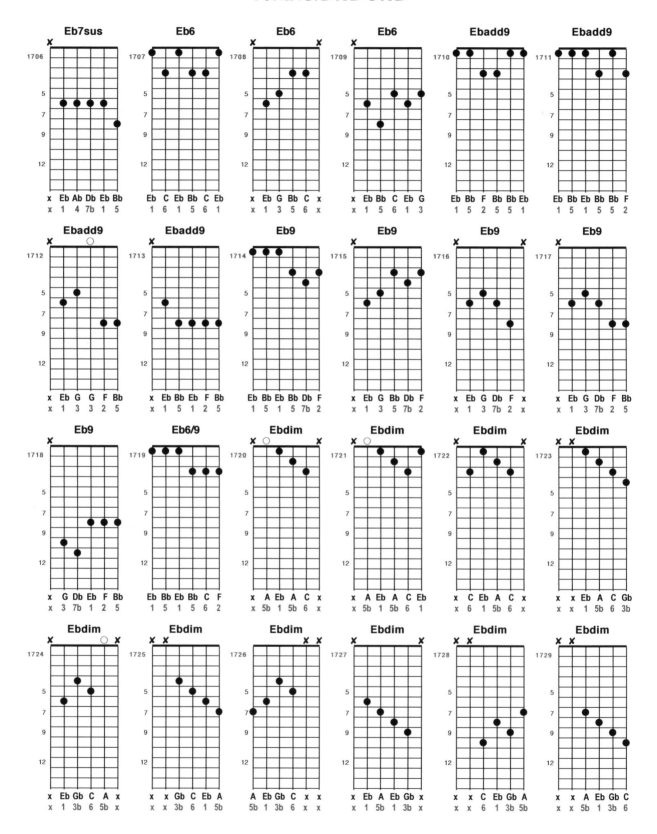

DADGAD Guitar Chords
TUNING: DADGAD

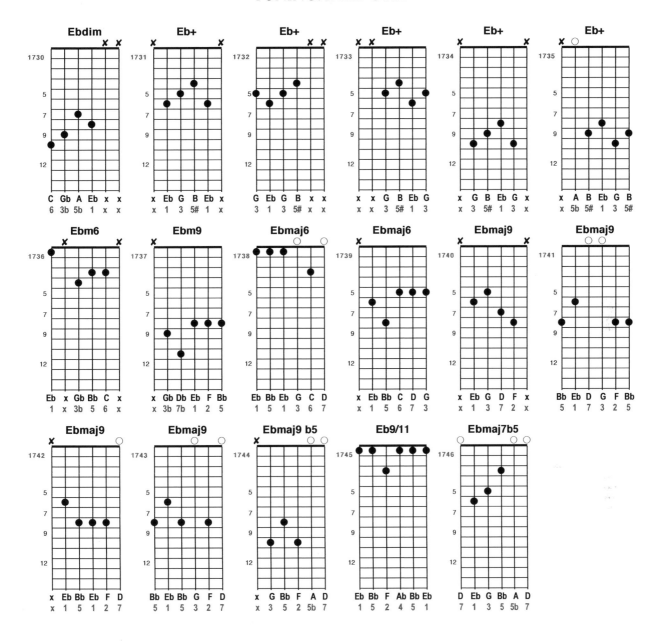

DADGAD Guitar Chords
TUNING: *D A D G A D*

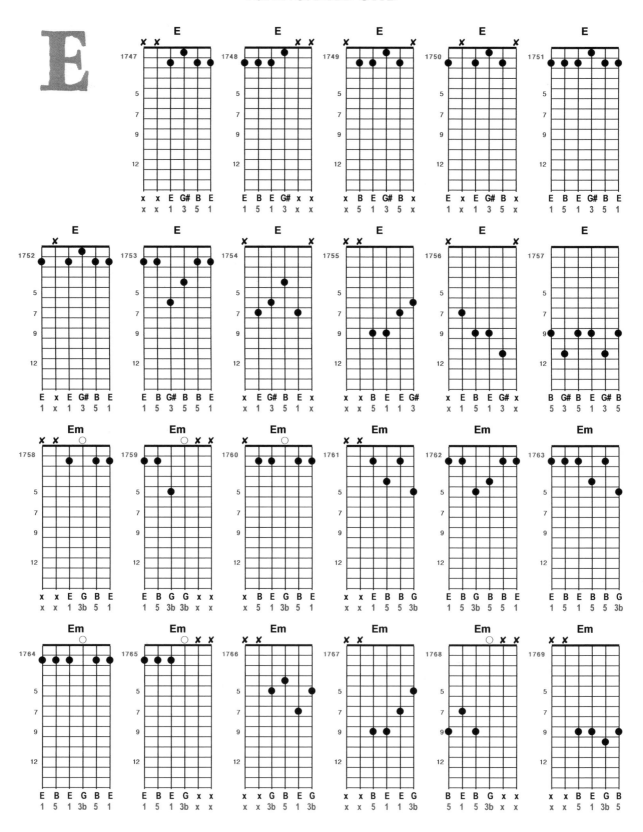

94

DADGAD Guitar Chords
TUNING: D A D G A D

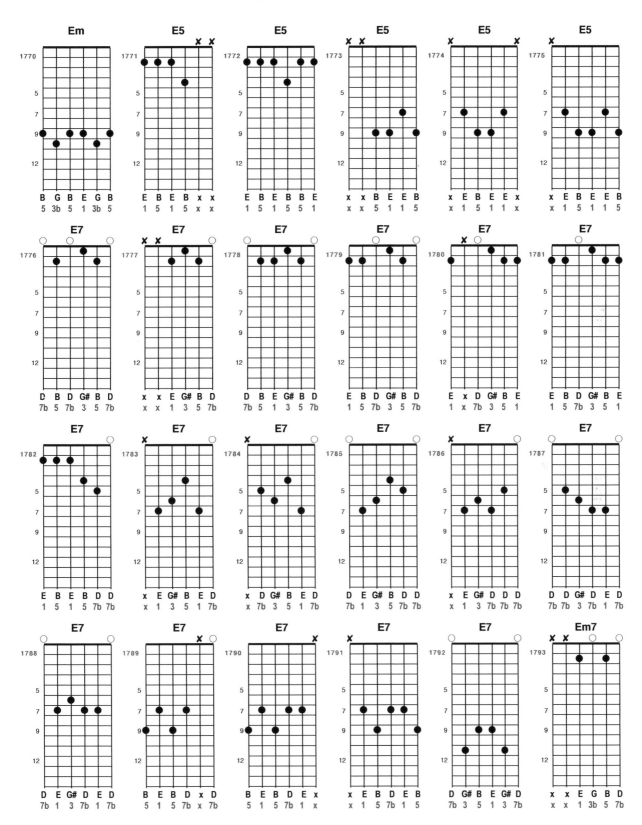

DADGAD Guitar Chords
TUNING: D A D G A D

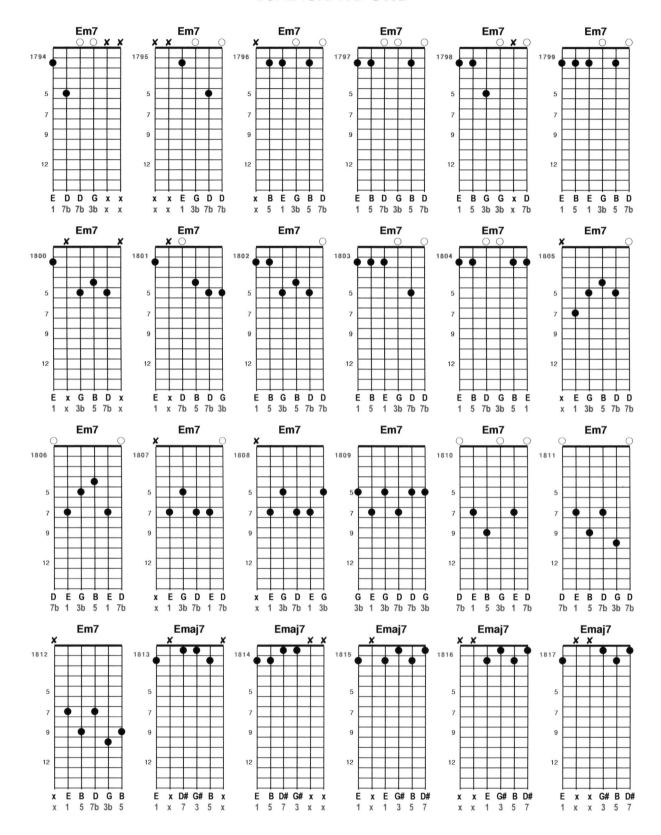

96

DADGAD Guitar Chords
TUNING: D A D G A D

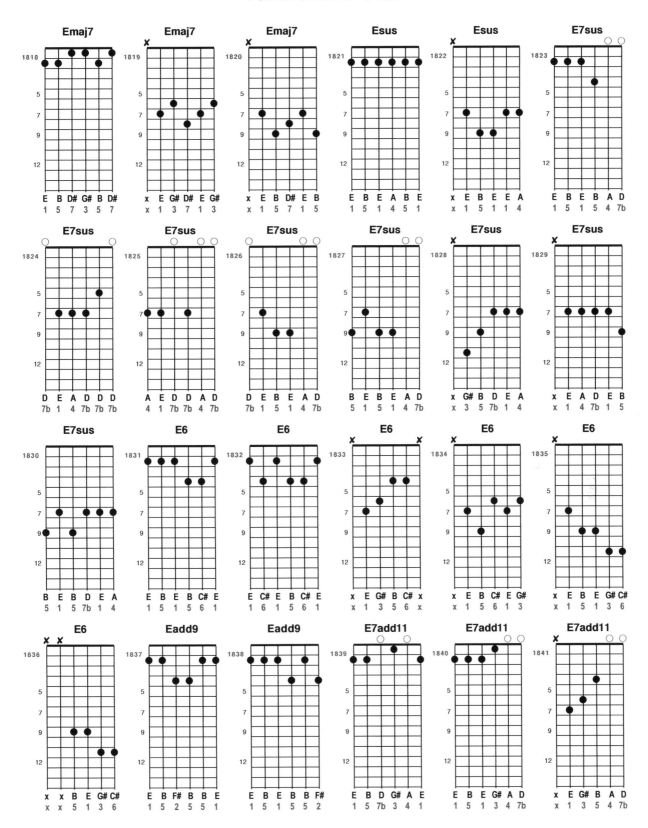

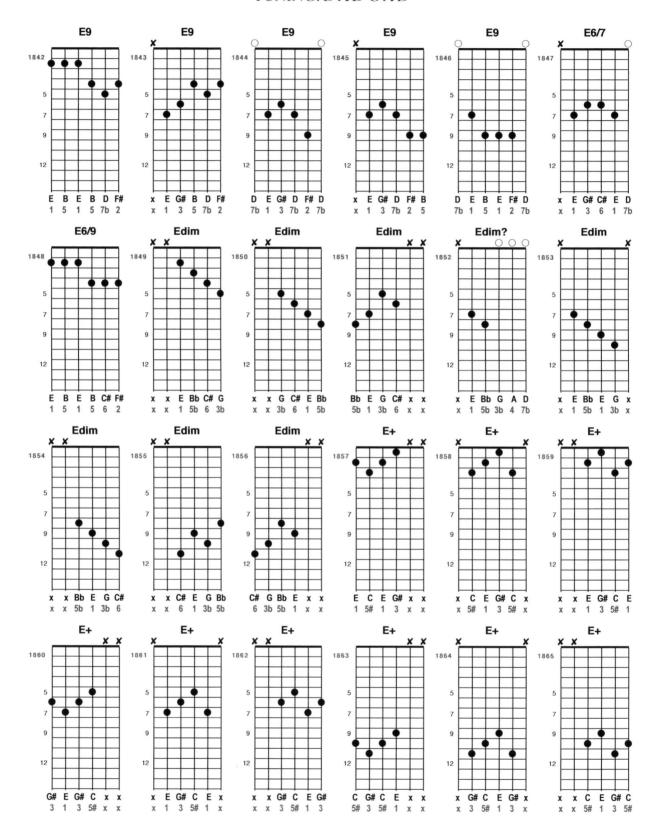

DADGAD Guitar Chords
TUNING: D A D G A D

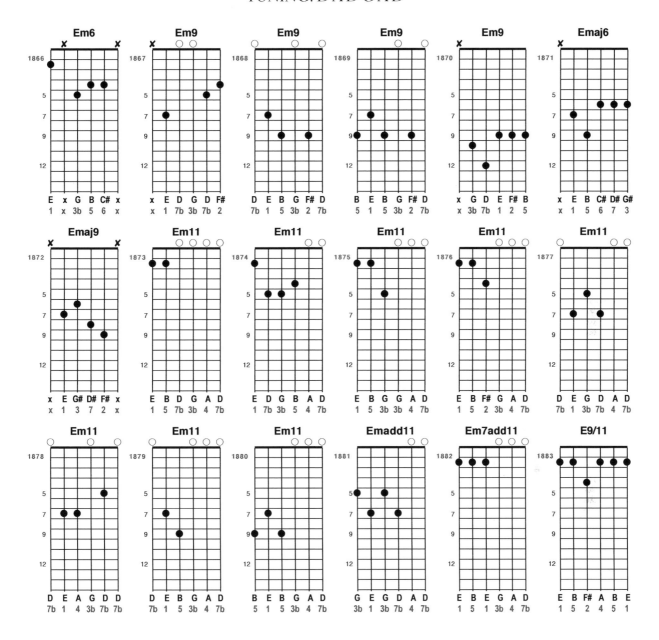

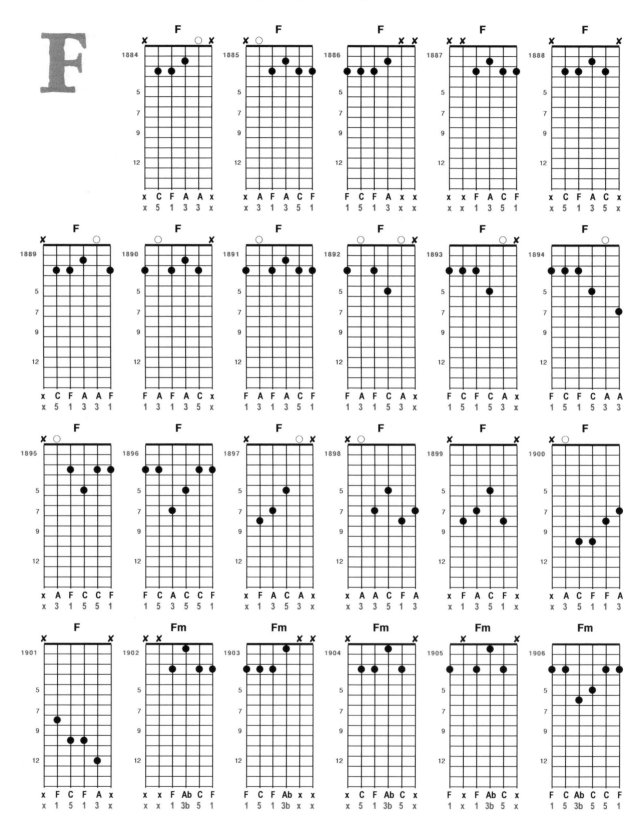

DADGAD Guitar Chords
TUNING: DADGAD

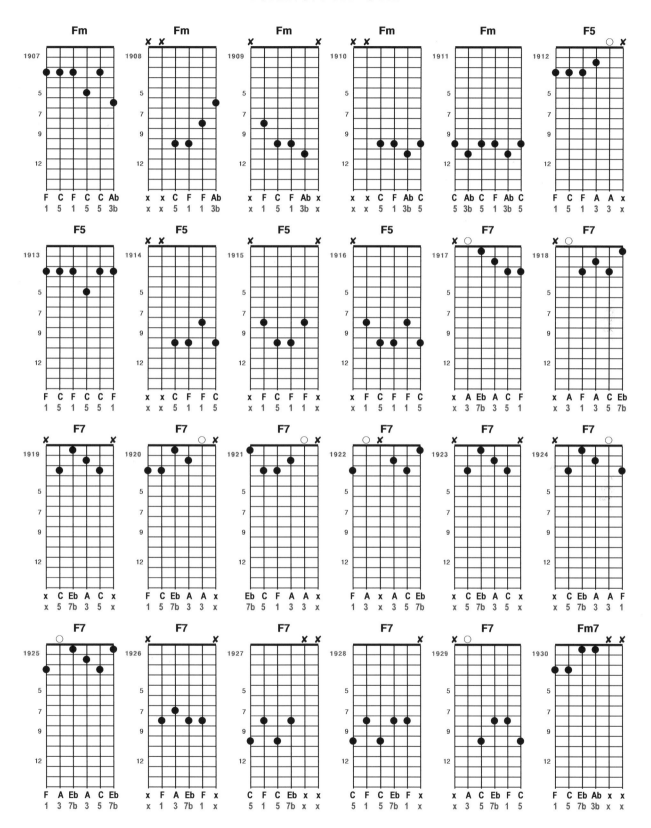

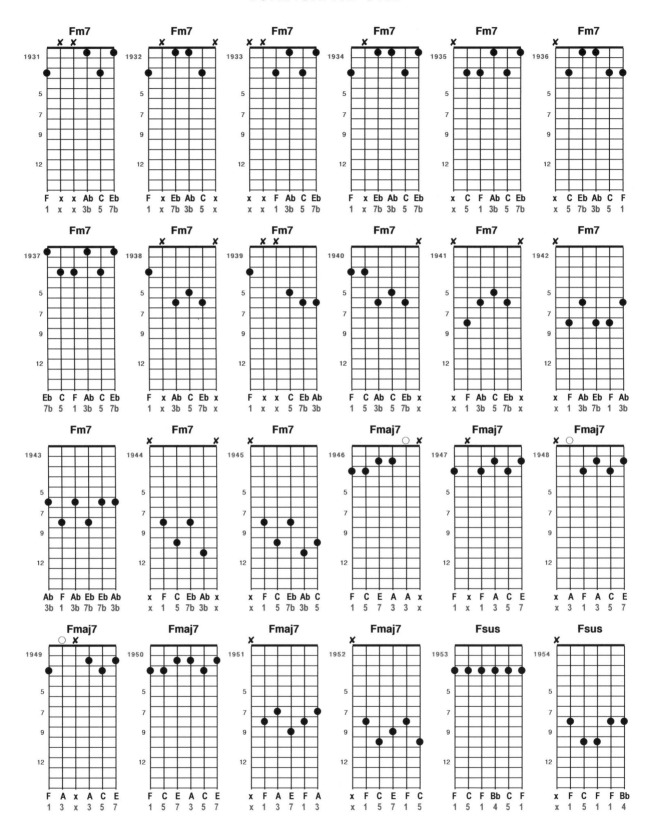

TUNING: D A D G A D

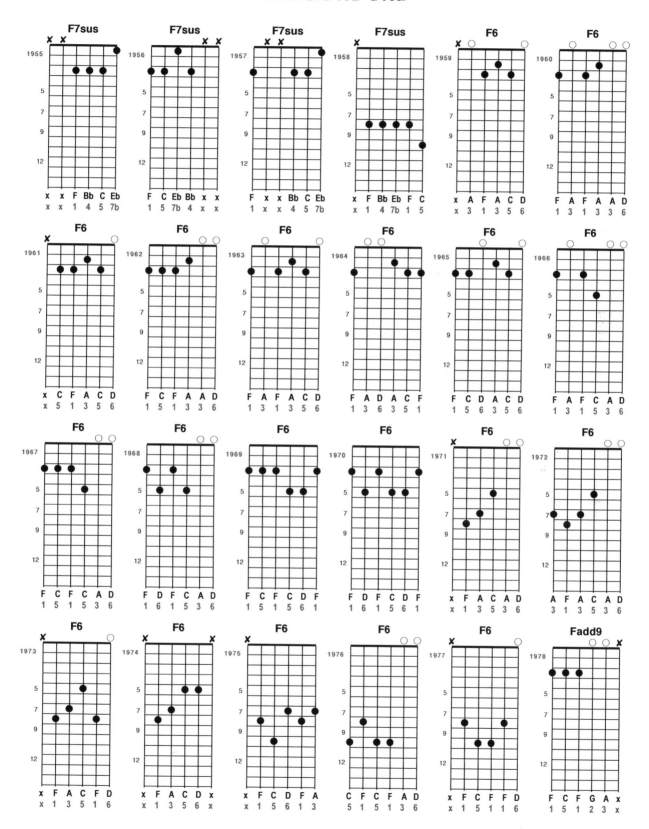

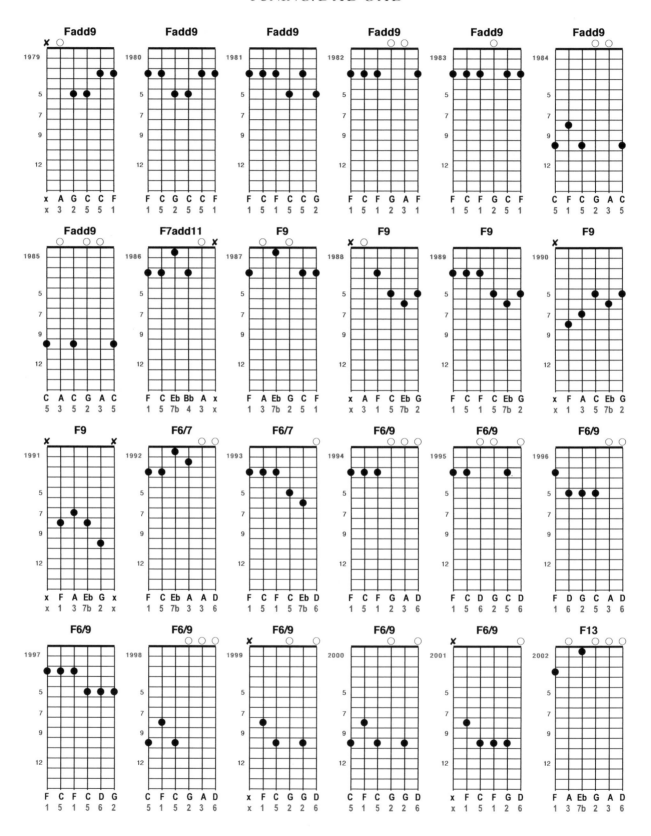

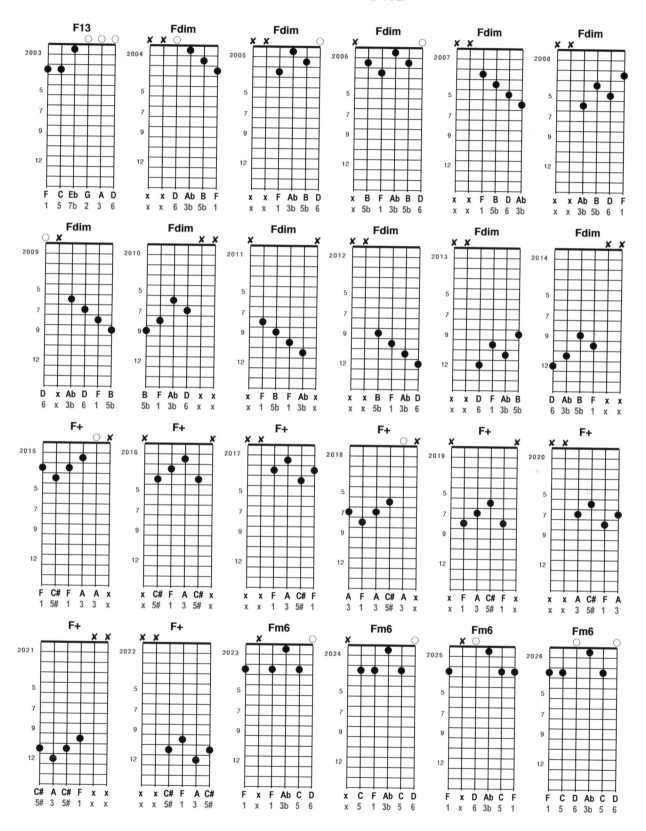

DADGAD Guitar Chords
TUNING: D A D G A D

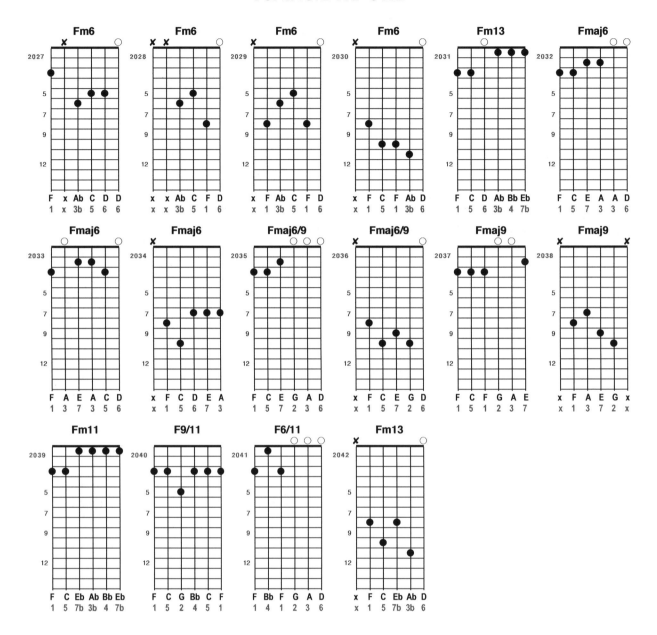

DADGAD Guitar Chords
TUNING: DADGAD

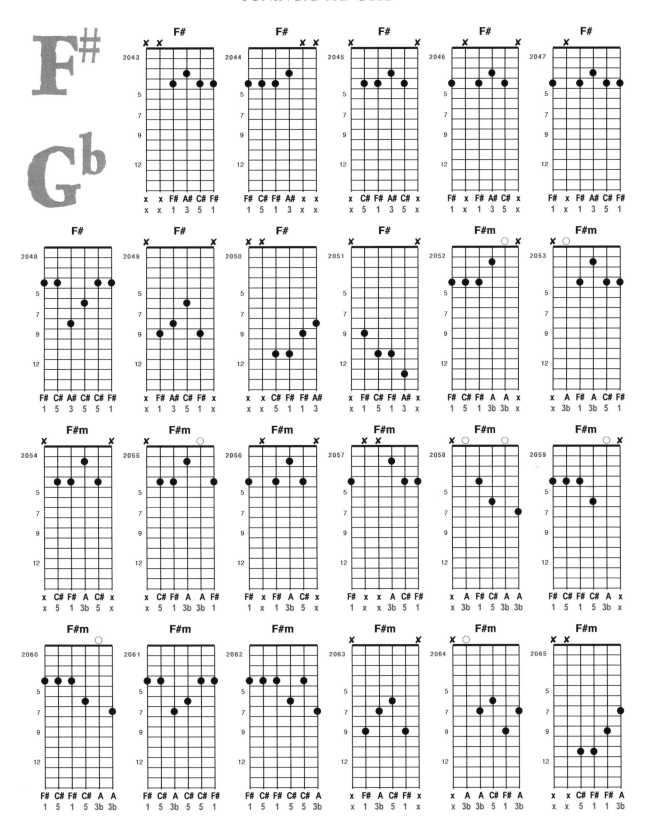

107

DADGAD Guitar Chords
TUNING: D A D G A D

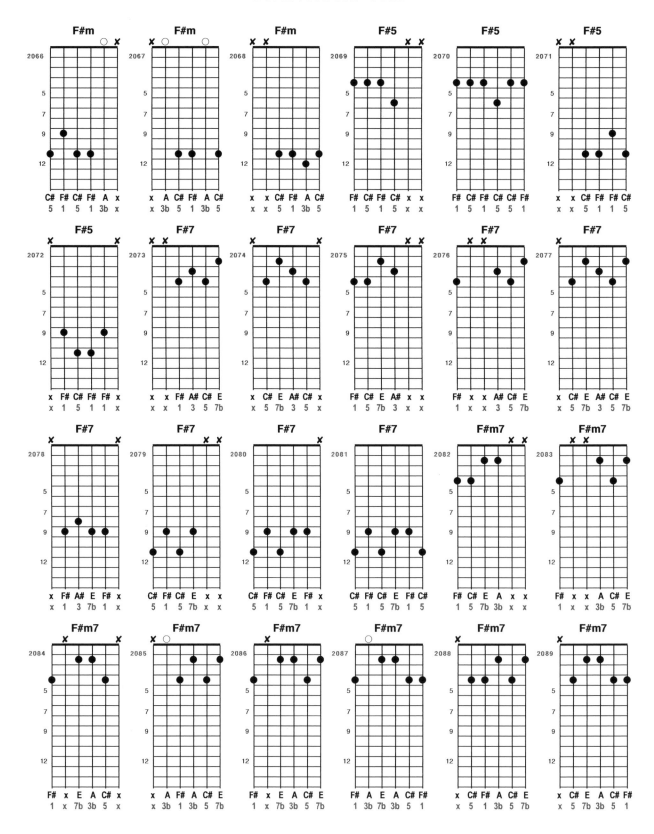

DADGAD Guitar Chords

TUNING: D A D G A D

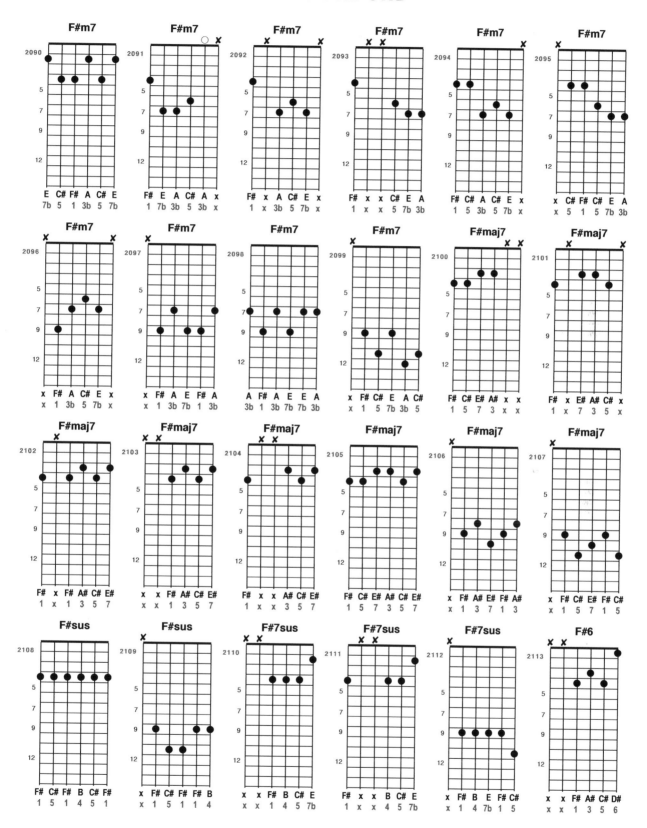

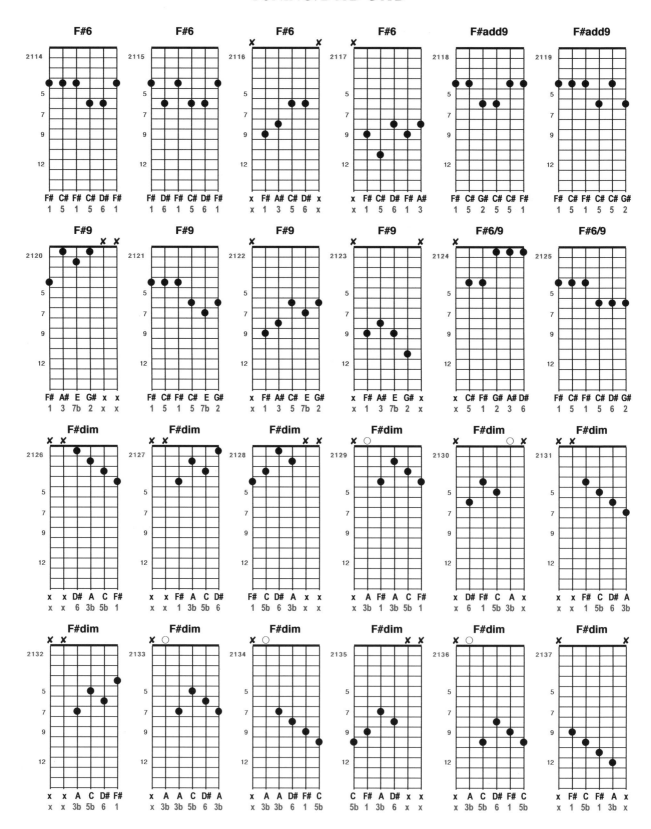

DADGAD Guitar Chords

TUNING: DADGAD

Tuning: DADGAD   Capo: 000000

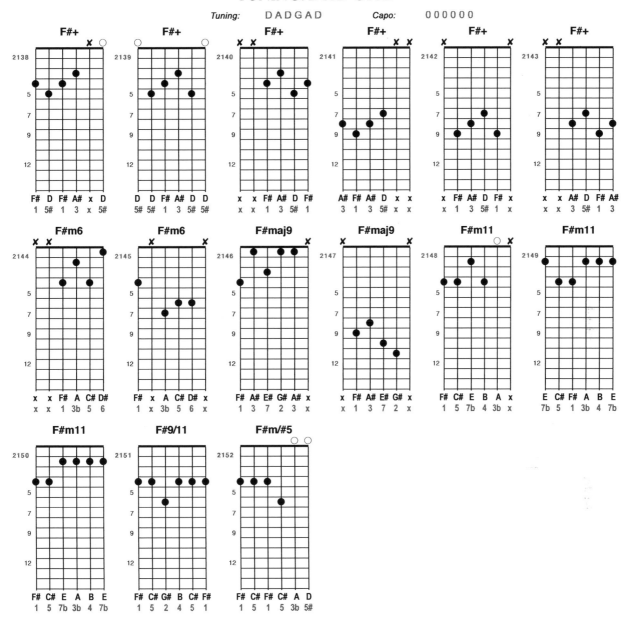

DADGAD Guitar Chords
TUNING: D A D G A D

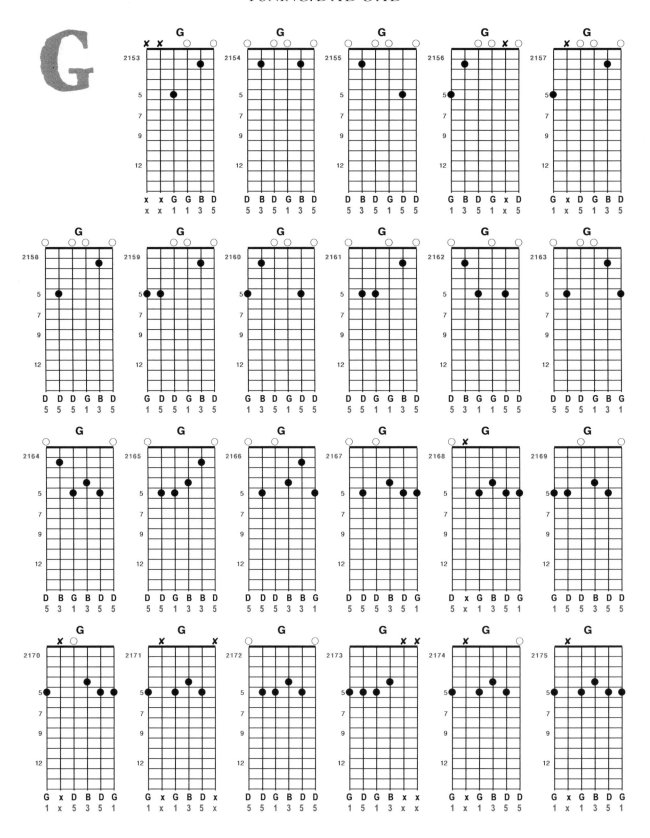

DADGAD Guitar Chords
TUNING: DADGAD

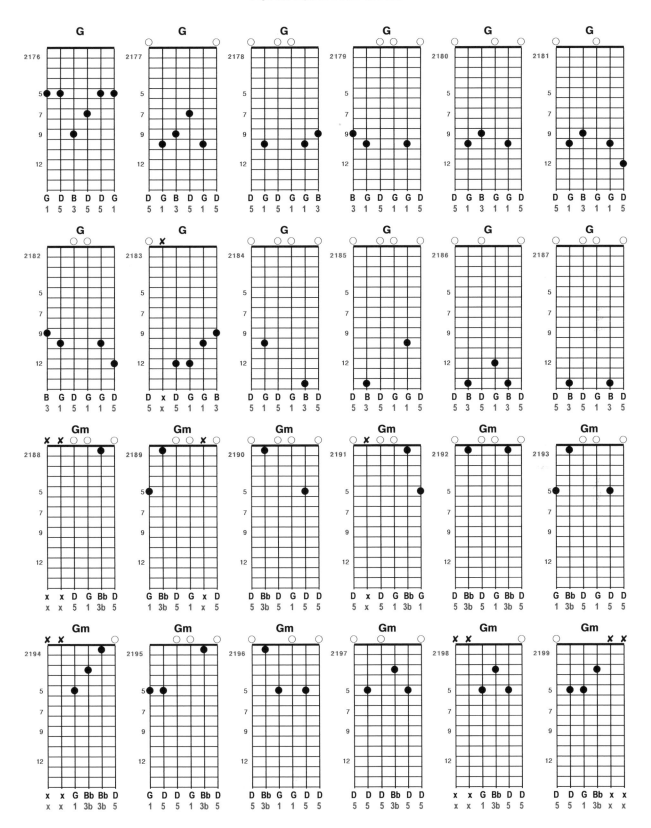

113

DADGAD Guitar Chords
TUNING: D A D G A D

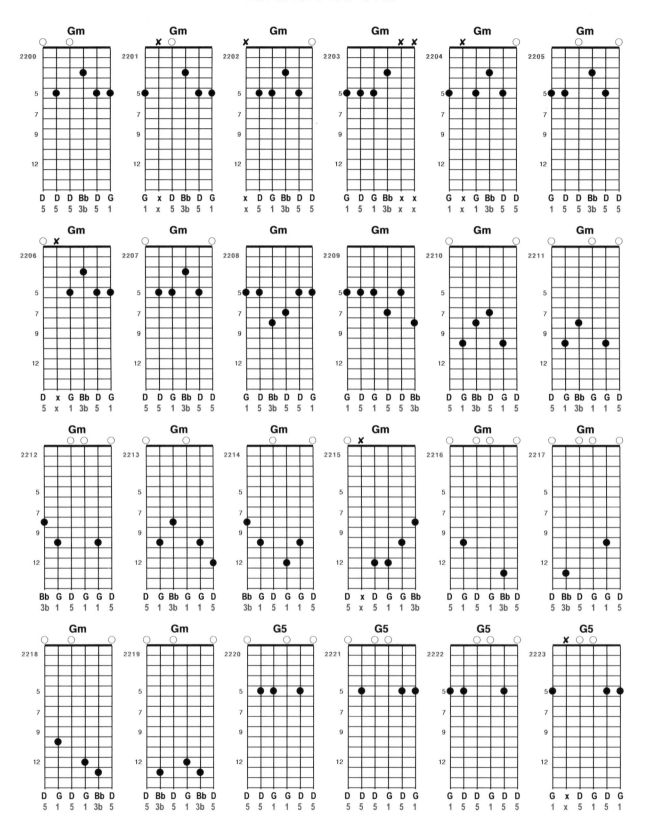

DADGAD Guitar Chords
TUNING: D A D G A D

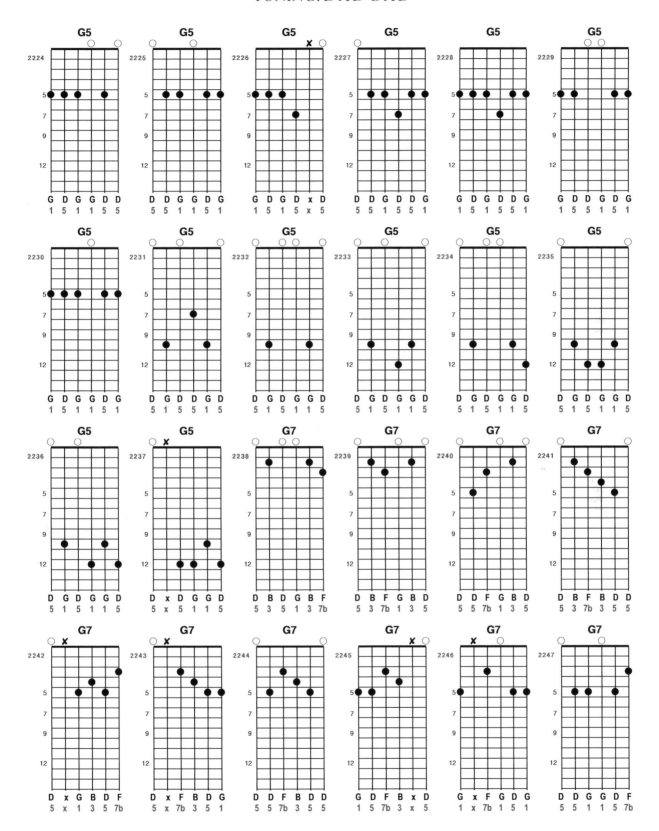

115

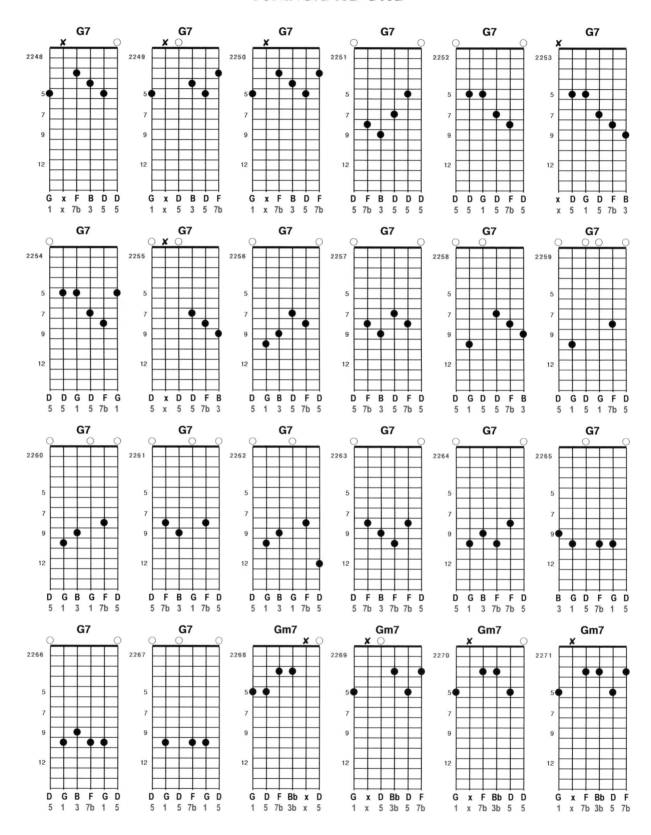

DADGAD Guitar Chords
TUNING: DADGAD

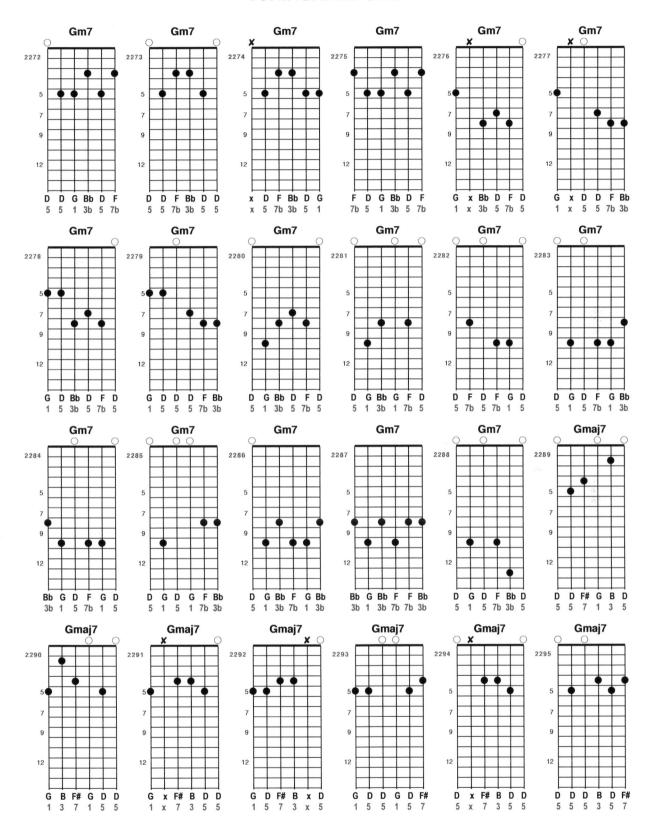

DADGAD Guitar Chords
TUNING: DADGAD

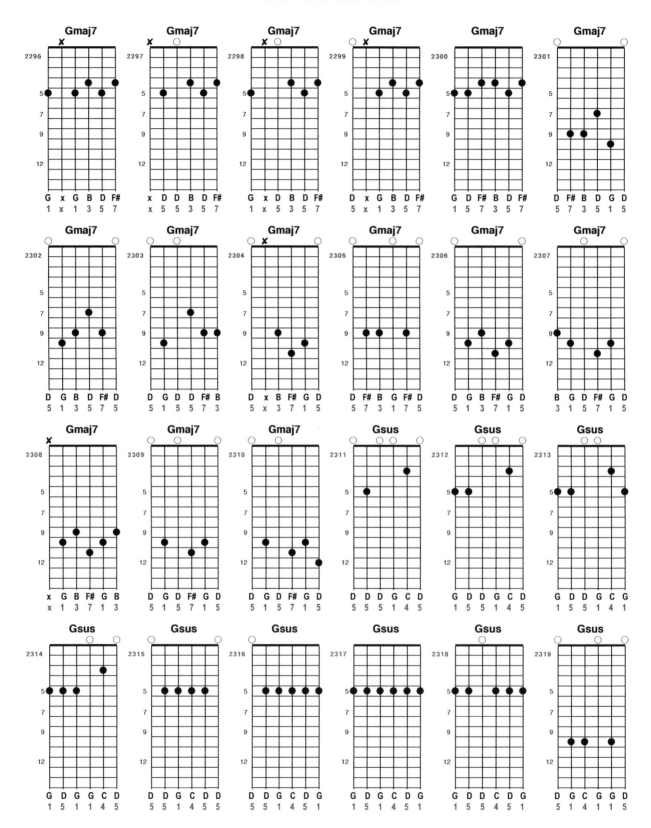

DADGAD Guitar Chords
TUNING: D A D G A D

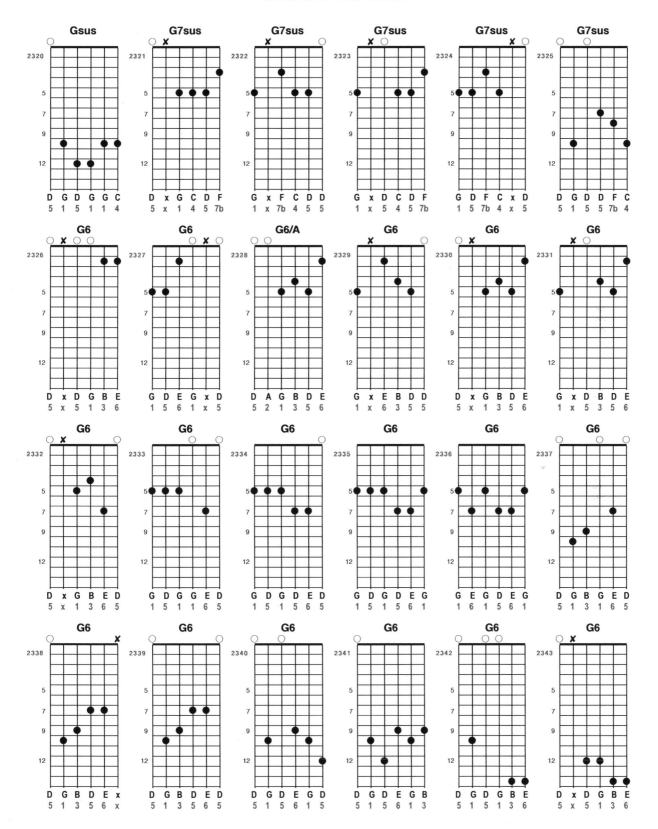

DADGAD Guitar Chords
TUNING: D A D G A D

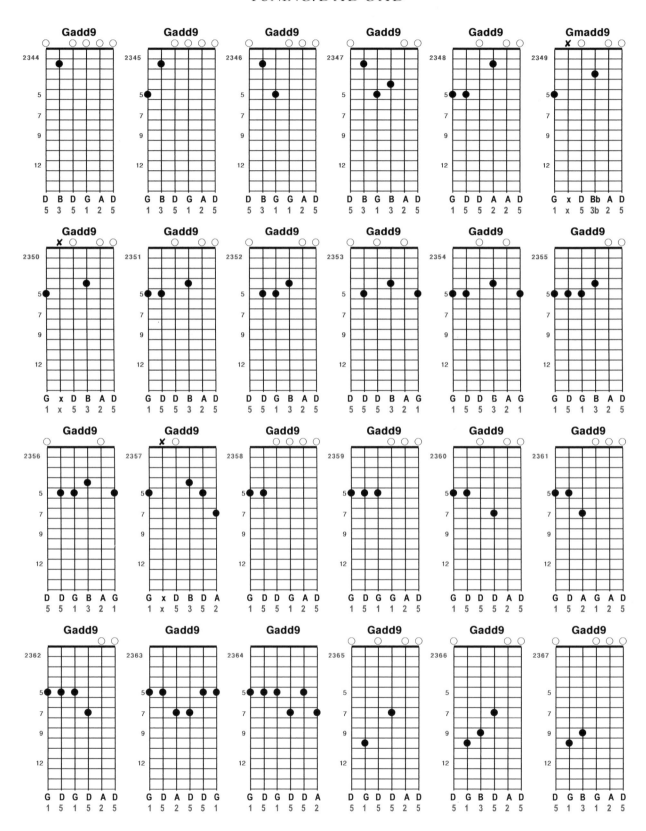

DADGAD Guitar Chords
TUNING: DADGAD

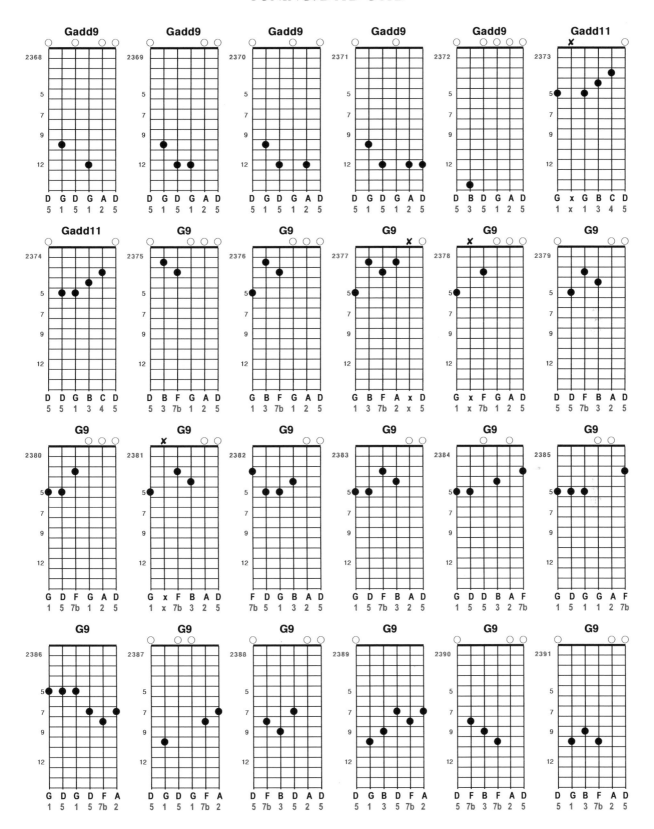

DADGAD Guitar Chords
TUNING: D A D G A D

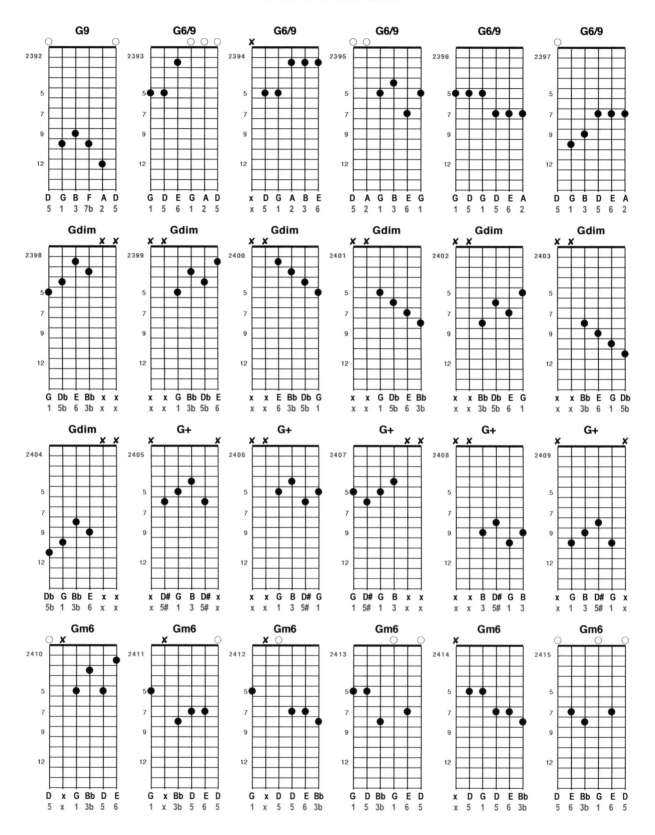

TUNING: D A D G A D

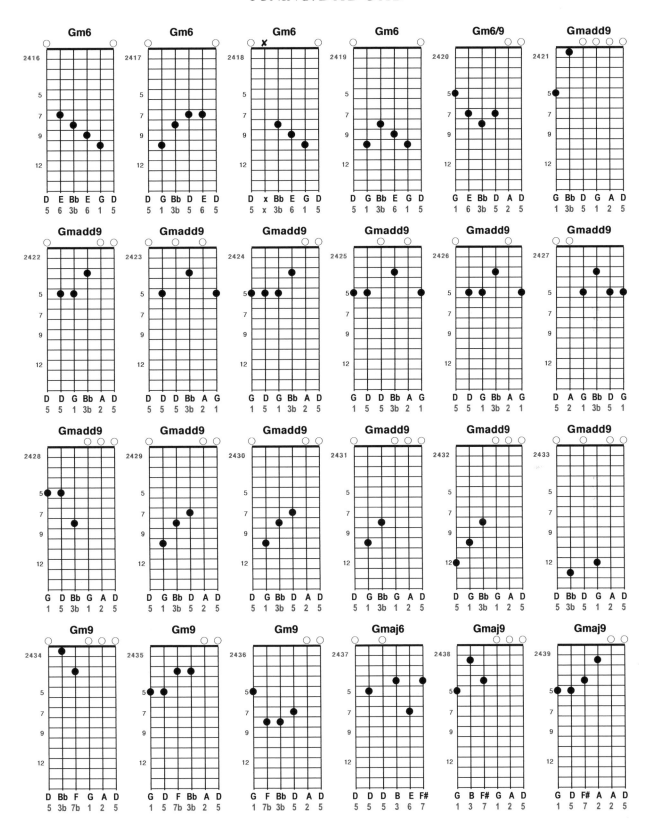

DADGAD Guitar Chords
TUNING: D A D G A D

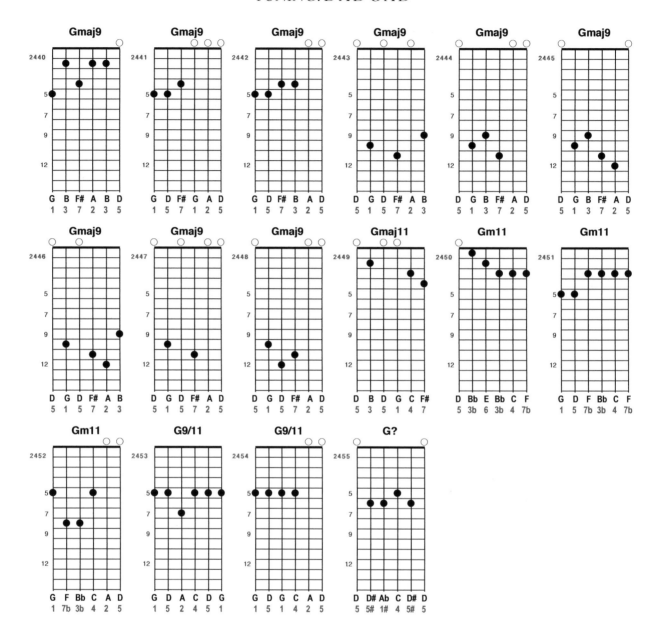

TUNING: DADGAD

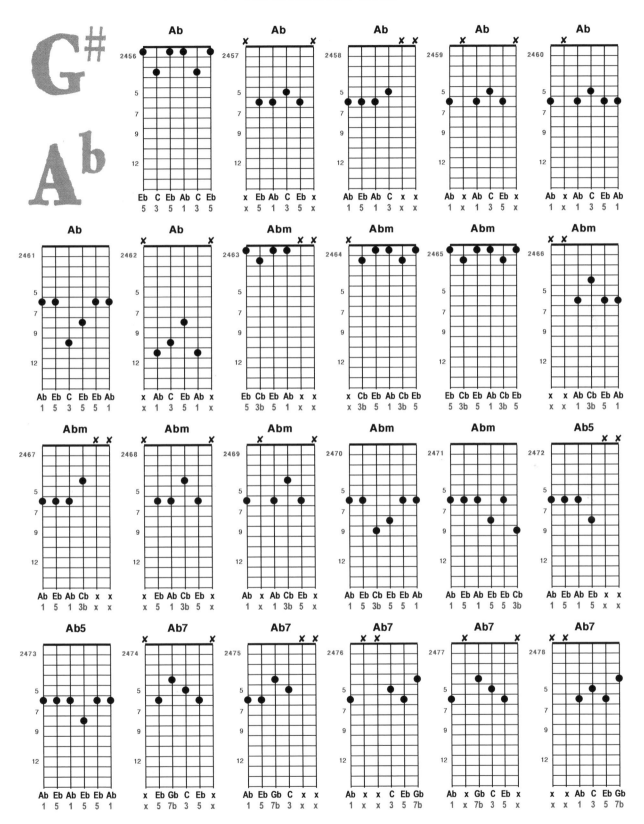

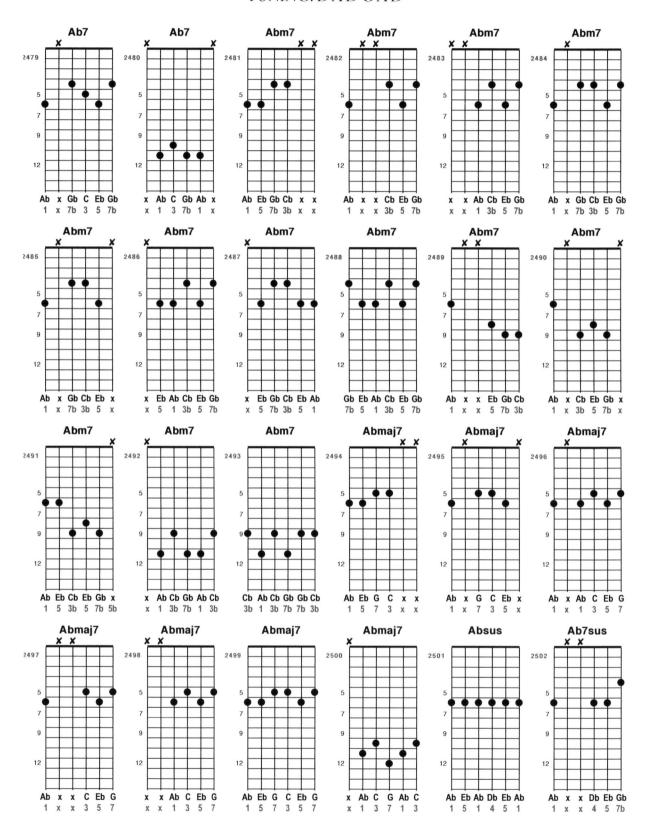

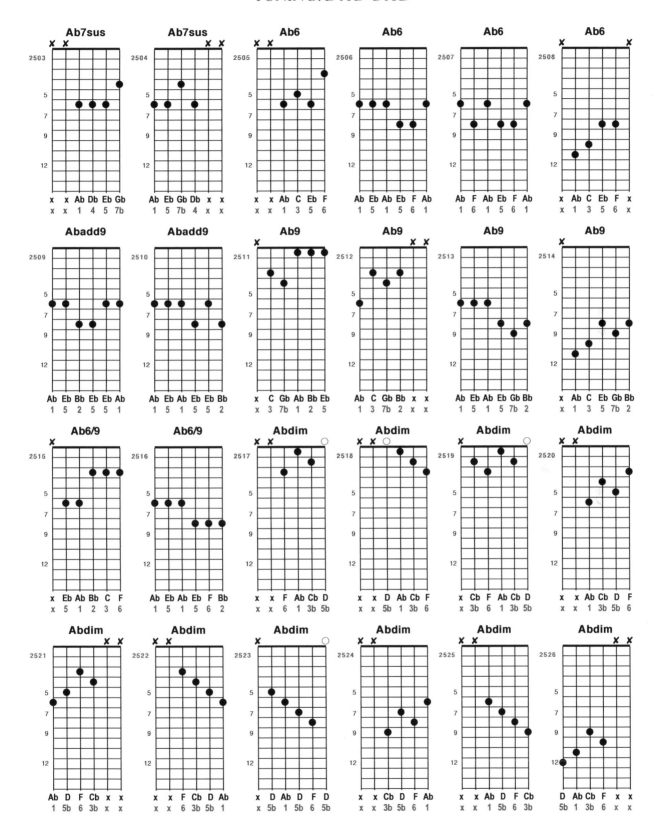

DADGAD Guitar Chords
TUNING: D A D G A D

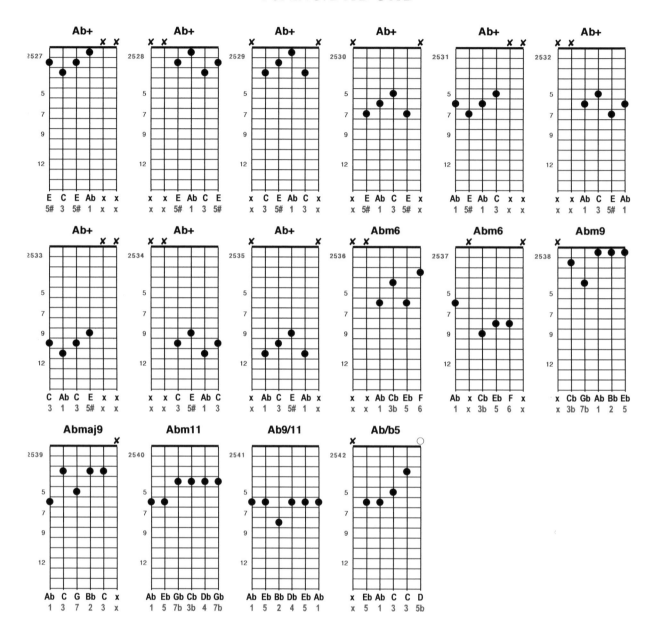

Appendix: About Chord Structure

About Sharps and Flats

Most of us know that D# (D-*sharp*) and E♭ (E-*flat*) are two different names for the same musical note that lies between D and E. There is even a fancy word for it: they are called "*enharmonic equivalents.*" On the piano, sharps and flats are black keys, while white keys have simple letter names. The naming system makes sense to a pianist who reads music, but is quite confusing to a troubadour guitarist, whose frets are the same color and who likely plays by ear.

Unfortunately, the musical notation system is most confusing to guitar troubadours, who happen to be the largest group of people playing musical instruments, so it is worth taking a little time to explain things.

When the word *sharp* or *flat* is used as a verb, it means to move up or down in pitch, and usually refers to an upward move of a single increment, which would be the next key on the piano or the next fret up the guitar neck. "*Sharp that note, please*" would tell you to move to the next higher note. A singer or violin player might also produce a note that is *flat*, which means it's too low in pitch by any amount. A guitar that is tuned *sharp* would mean that all the strings are tighter than normal. In a guitar chord situation we might mention the sharp fifth (#5) note of a C scale, which means that the normal 5th (G) is sharped up to G#. If we sharp a Bb it becomes a B.

It takes some study of music to understand why this dual-naming is done. The choice of whether to call a note A# or Bb is really determined in the musical context of a particular piece of music. In a guitar chord book, there is no context, so it is a little arbitrary what to name things. I called the section after C in this book C#, while others, especially those who are used to playing jazz with horns (who always play in flat keys like F, Bb, Eb etc.) would have called it Db.

There are situations in music where a note is written as a double-sharp or double-flat, and there is such as thing as a G##, or even a B# and a Cb, though it would seem that a B# would just be a C natural. (The 7th scale position in the key of G# is an F##.) There isn't a good reason to use double accidentals in this book. There is even a third symbol (these three symbols are collectively

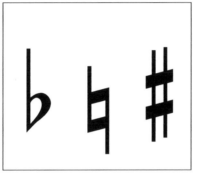

called accidentals) known as the "natural." A natural symbol (♮) indicates that the musician is to ignore the flat or sharp symbol on that staff line temporarily. So a piece of music in G, that usually had all F's sharped to F#, might have an F natural note in it, which is the flat 7th note of the G scale, because the F# is the usual 7th note. Understanding that "flatting an F sharp note yields an F natural" is precisely the kind of thing that happens all the time in music, but this language is confusing to a campfire musician. Naturals are used commonly in sheet music because of the parameters imposed by the key signature at the beginning of each line of music, but they are not used in chord diagrams, and don't appear in this book.

It is painfully clumsy to call a note "D-sharp or E-flat" every time you mention it, and what is usually done is determined by a hierarchy of the so-called order of sharps and order of flats. F is the key that uses only one flatted note (black key) in its major scale, so to ensure that the F scale includes each of the 7 letters once and only once, its scale is written F-G-A-Bb-C-D-E-F. So "A-sharp" is much less commonly used for the note between A and B, and it is usually called "B flat." The key of Bb is the next most complex "flat key" and it has both a Bb and an Eb in its scale. For the same reason, we hear people talk about Eb much more than D#.

Likewise, among guitarists, F# and C# are used much more often than their enharmonic equivalents Gb or Db, and most musicians in conversation, instruction books or chord books, will use the more common of the 2 names. The order of flats is B-E-A-D-G-C and the order of sharps is F-C-G-D-A-E-B. This works reasonably well, until you go to the "farther" keys like C# and you will always reach some confusion about what to call some things. Choosing between the key name C# or Db can be fuzzy. In this book I used C#, because most guitarists think in sharps and not flats. This means that the musical 3rd of that scale is an E#. My system does not handle the augmented chord, where the #5 note should be a G## and my charts call it an A. If I called the key Db then the flat 7 note in a lot of chords would be a Cb, and the 5b in a diminished chord would be an Abb. There are similar problems in the keys of F# and G#.

Rather than calling every accidental by 2 names, or doing something radical like calling every accidental a sharp, which makes logical but not musical sense, I chose to use the more common names for each chord and for the notes in the chord. The point of this book is to show you where your fingers go on the fretboard, and to help you understand the musical value of each note in the chord. If you are a novice troubadour, and are using this book, be aware that there is such a thing a D# chord, though you are generally better off calling it an Eb.

A final thought: there are special typographic symbols for sharp ♯ and flat ♭, but I have chosen for the sake of simplicity in typesetting this book to just use a lower case B (b) for the flat symbol, even though I know there is a slightly different symbol. The flat and sharp symbols don't occur in normal typefaces, and it is very awkward to typeset them, especially in sentences like this, and the fonts used in e-books sometimes don't even allow them and they disturb the line spacing in the paragraphs that use them.

About Naming Guitar Chords

Professors of music probably cringe when we guitarists start talking guitar chord theory, since a lot of what we do is a little contrary to the way Western music has been taught for centuries. It is only because of the proliferation and dominance of guitars in recent decades in American music that there has been a push to use and name guitar chords. Composers and pianists got by for centuries without doing what we all do now, which is to analyze the structure of all our chords, and to catalog and categorize them. They thought more in terms of "lines" and harmony, and not really "chords."

Only some chords have names, and people don't agree on the names or the notation systems used for chords that have been named. **Chords may have more than one name**, which is also confusing when you are compiling a book of guitar chords, and everyone who makes guitar chord books makes up names and uses all sorts of different symbols and terminology. It seems to be all organized, but it is in many ways a lawless jungle.

First We Name The Notes

The naming system for musical notes makes more sense

Bear in mind that not all chord have common names, there are different names, symbols, abbreviations and nicknames for chords, and not all chords will actually contain every one of the notes in their "spelling." There are hundreds of ways to rearrange the notes in every type of chord. Knowing which notes can be doubled or omitted, and how to use the chords in musical situations is something that takes a lifetime to learn.

once you have used it for a while, but it is confusing to a beginner, especially if you never studied piano and are a recreational guitarist. The piano and the notation system evolved together, and the whole notation system really doesn't make sense on just a guitar. The idea that some of the notes have 2 names is both useful and hard to swallow at first. The note between F and G is sometimes called F# and sometimes Gb. *Hmmm.*

In Western music, the octave is divided into 12 equal pieces called half-steps or semi-tones, or on guitar, frets. The 12th fret of a stringed instrument has the same name as the open string, and it is 1/2 the string length exactly. (The ratio of the length of each fret of a guitar to the adjacent fret is the 12th root of 2, a thoroughly irrational number.) There is a certain amount of numerological mystery to all this, and most people who have studied either math or music know about the mysterious relationship of integers to music. The harmonic series: 1/2, 1/3, 1/4, 1/5, 1/6 etc has a lot to do with music, and represents the overtones of vibrating objects. The numbers 5, 7 and 12 appear a lot in musical ideas.

There are only 7 notes in most scales, and they are given the 7 letter names from A to G, with the accidentals (sharps & flats) sprinkled in. The only thing you really have to memorize is that there are no sharps or flats between B and C, and between E and F. Remember the piano keyboard layout, where some white keys are adjacent but most aren't. The rest of chord theory you can figure out from some simple rules.

Next We Look At The Intervals

The system for describing how each chord is built used to be based on what are called intervals, which is the musical distance between 2 notes. On a one-dimensional instrument like the piano it makes total sense to think this way. Traditional music theory talks of combining 2 intervals to make a 3-note chord, and stacking up larger groups of intervals, triads and even *tetrachords* (4-note chords) to build the more complex and extended chords. **We don't really need to know about intervals to use this book, and guitarists really don't think in terms of them, so I'll be brief here.**

Intervals are given names according to how many

consecutive letters they span, which can be confusing. Any interval that spans the letter names C to D is a second, though it might be C-D (also a major 2nd) Cb-Db (major 2nd), C-Db (minor 2nd), C#-D (minor 2nd), C#-D# (major 2nd). Intervals get names: unison, 2nd, 3rd, 4th etc, and there are modifiers: *perfect, augmented,* and *diminished* for unisons, octaves, 4ths and 5ths, and *major* or *minor* for 2nd, 3rd, 6th or 7^{th}s. All intervals can be augmented. All intervals but the unison can be diminished. Only seconds, thirds, sixths, and sevenths can be major or minor. Got it? Maybe there is a reason this system for describing chord structure isn't universal.

Every chord can be described as a series of intervals. A *major triad* (3 notes) is made by stacking up 2 intervals of 4 and then 3 half steps (frets), known as a major 3rd plus a minor 3rd. Reversing the order of these two intervals builds a *minor triad.* Two minor 3rds stacked up makes a *diminished triad,* and two major 3rds create an *augmented triad.* Intervals make sense and are quite visual on the piano keyboard, where letter names are white keys and accidentals are black keys and on paper, since a staff is a linear representation of pitch.

INTERVAL	Steps	Example
perfect unison	0	C-C
augmented unison	1	C-C#
minor 2nd	1	C-Db
major 2nd	2	C-D
augmented 2nd	3	C-D#
minor 3rd	3	C-Eb
major 3rd	4	C-E
augmented 3rd	5	C-E#
diminished 4th	4	C-Fb
perfect 4th	5	C-F
augmented 4th	6	C-F#
diminished 5th	6	C-Gb
perfect 5th	7	C-G
augmented 5th	8	C-G#
minor 6th	8	C-Ab
major 6th	9	C-A
augmented 6th	10	C-A#
minor 7th	10	C-Bb
major seventh	11	C-Bb
octave	12	C-C

Trouble is, when we play a ninth chord on guitar, we are not playing the notes in numerical order– we play them the way we can. Our 9th chord might not have a 5th and it might have 2 of them, and it might have the 5th on the bottom and it might not.

Describing 6-string guitar chords with intervals is extremely messy, and not that helpful to a guitarist in explaining what is going on musically, because the guitar is not linear like a piano keyboard. Look at the 50-somedifferent D chords in this book. They all have a different sequence of intervals that make them up. But they all are made up of the same 3 notes: D-F#-A.

The interval-based system of describing chords is too clumsy to describe thousands of guitar chords, so a simpler but also slightly illogical numerical system is employed that uses the major scale numbers 1 through 7 combined with sharps and flats to mark the position of each note. I use this in this book, and so do most guitar chord publications.

The 12 Major Scales

Even if you play music that never uses a major scale, you'll still use the major scale numbers to describe the notes in the chords. That's how it is usually done, and it is what all the numbers in chord names and underneath each chord in this book are about. You need to at least understand what a *major scale* is.

A scale is nothing more than a group of notes arranged in order of pitch. There are dozens, possibly hundreds of kinds of scales that are associated with the various kinds of music in the world, and an exhaustive discussion of them is beyond the scope of this book.

In a so-called major scale, which is just one type of scale, the 7 notes are separated by half-steps (frets) in the pattern 2-2-1-2-2-2-1. Start on any guitar string, and climb up frets in this order, you'll finish at fret 12, and you'll hear a *do-re-mi* major scale. Remember this pattern.

There is a major scale built on each of the 12 note names, and since 5 of the 12 note names have dual names, we could map out 17 major scales instead of just 12.

Because Eb is less clumsy than D#, and Bb is much more manageable than A#, we rarely hear about the key or the scale of A# or D#. The notes D# and A# appear in some of chords we play but we don't play in those keys. This is confusing. The B major 7th chord has an A# note in it, and the F#m chord has a D# note in it.

Guitars normally play in the keys of C, G, D, A and E, which are all "sharp keys." Jazz evolved with a lot of horns, which play in "flat keys" like Bb and Eb. Jazz theory uses a lot more flats, and in guitar chord theory that is not part of a jazz curriculum, we have a tendency to just use sharps and kind of ignore flats. This is why I use C# instead of Db. You could almost get by in guitar by just calling every accidental a sharp. So I put the Db scale next to the C# scale.

Let's have a look at the major scales, since these generate

all the chord spellings in the book. **Each letter name appears once and only once in each scale.** This is a big part of the reason why the sharps and flats are used.

Now We Can Map the Chord Structures

The major chord (which we previously described as an interval of a major 3rd plus a minor 3rd stacked on a note...) can also be defined as the 1st, 3rd and 5th notes of a major scale. The C major chord is the 1-3-5 notes of the first row in the scales chart (previous page), which is the notes C-E-G. Likewise, a D chord has the 1-3-5 notes of the D scale (see chart) which means D-F#-A. Each other type of chord also has a numeric spelling, as shown in the next chart.

What comes next is a little confusing... When we play in the key of G, our three most common chords are G-C-D, referred to as the *tonic* (1or I) the *sub-dominant* (4 or IV) and the *dominant* (5 or V.) The names of those chords come from the G scale, since we are playing in the key of G. The 1-4-5 positions of the G scale are G-C-D.

The Basic Major Scales (both C# and Db are shown)

Root 1	2	3	4	5	6	7	sharps/ flats
C	D	E	F	G	A	B	none
C#	D#	E#	F#	G#	A#	B#	7#
Db	Eb	F	Gb	Ab	Bb	C	5b
D	E	F#	G	A	B	C#	2#
Eb	F	G	Ab	Bb	C	D	3b
E	F#	G#	A	B	C#	D#	4#
F	G	A	Bb	C	D	E	1b
F#	G#	A#	B	C#	D#	E#	6#
G	A	B	C	D	E	F#	1#
Ab	Bb	C	Db	Eb	F	G	4b
A	B	C#	D	E	F#	G#	3#
Bb	C	D	Eb	F	G	A	2b
B	C#	D#	E	F#	G#	A#	5#

But each of those 3 chords is made up of 3 notes. The G chord itself is made up of the 1-3-5 notes (not the 1-4-5-- that was for chords, not notes) of the G scale, which are G-B-D. Look at all the G chords in this book-- they are all made up of various combinations of those 3 notes only. The C chord is the 1-3-5 notes (C-E-G) of the C scale and the D chord is likewise made up of the 1-3-5 (D-F#-A) notes of the D scale. This is confusing at first, to name the notes in every chord according to the major scale built on its root note name, regardless of what key the song is in.

There are of course lots of other types of chords in the world that are not in this book, and there are fuzzy and gray areas within certain types of chords.

An 11th chord, for example may have the 1-3-5-7-9-11 scale notes in it, and it may just have some of them. It's hard to know when to call it an 11th and when it is an "add11."

There will always be some chords where it is unclear what to call them, and ambiguous chords are often musically interesting and useful. When you get a chord with 5 or 6 notes in it, and you start scrambling the order and omitting notes, those same notes can often be understood as another kind of chord entirely. What the chord is named has everything to do with how it is used in a piece of music, and in a book like this they are not being used in specific songs, and are just "laboratory specimens."

The Order of Notes in a Chord

The real workings of chord theory are determined by how a chord is used in a piece of music, and studying them too closely out of context can be pointless. There are also a lot of examples of unusual voicings of chords that sound great in certain songs or as part of a progression of chords, but that might sound odd when played by themselves.

On guitar, we take what we can get, and we don't have the same choices of notes that pianists have for the order of notes. We may use a chord whose voicing is not ideal because it is all we can reach, and we may also push ourselves to play a hard fingering because it has a better or different sound.

The note names and scale degrees are shown for all the chords in this book. It offers an unprecedented look at the inner workings of all the chords.

Chord Name	Scale Degrees	*Example : C Scale*	Symbol or Abbrev.
major	1 - 3 - 5	C-E-G	C, Cmaj C△
minor	1 - 3^b - 5	C-E^b-G	Cm C-
modal	1 - 5	C-G	C5
diminished (dim7)	1 - 3^b - 5^b or 1-3^b-5^b-7bb (6)	C-E^b-G^b B^{bb} (A)	Cdim or C°
augmented	1 - 3# - 5#	C-F-G#	C+, Caug
suspended fourth	1 - 4 - 5	C-F-G	Csus, Csus4
sixth (added sixth)	1 - 3 - 5 - 6	C-E-G-A	C6
(dominant) seventh	1 - 3 - 5 - 7b	C-E-G-Bb	C7 Cdom7
major seventh	1 - 3 - 5 - 7	C-E-G-B	Cmaj7 Cma7 CM7 CMa7 C j7 C△7 C△
minor seventh	1 - 3^b - 5 -7b	C-E^b-G-Bb	Cm7 C-7
seventh suspended	1 - 4 - 5 - 7b	C-F-G-Bb	C7sus, C7sus4
add nine	1 - 3 - 5 - 2	C-E-G-D	Cadd9 , Csus2
minor add nine	1 - 3b - 5 - 2	C-Eb-G-D	Cmadd9
add eleven	1 - 3 - 5 - 4	C-E-G-F	Cadd11, Cadd4
minor add eleven	1 - 3b - 5 - 4	C-Eb-G-F	Cmadd11
(dominant) ninth	1 - 3 - 5 - 7b - 2	C-E-G-Bb-D	C9
major ninth	1 - 3 - 5 - 7 - 2	C-E-G-B-D	Cmaj9, Cma9, CM9 C j9 C△9
minor ninth	1 - 3b - 5 - 7b - 2	C-Eb-G-Bb-D	Cm9
major sixth	1 - 3 - 5 - 6 - 7	C-E-G-B-A	Cmaj6, Cma6, CM6 C j6 C△6
minor sixth	1 - 3b - 5 - 6	C-E^b-G-A	Cm6
6/7 (dominant sixth)	1 - 3 - 5 - 6 - 7b	C-E-G-Bb-A	C6/7
6/9	1 - 3 - 5 - 6 - 2	C-E-G-A-D	C6/9
eleventh	1 - 3 - 5 - 7b- 2- 4	C-E-G-Bb-D-F	C11
major eleventh	1 - 3 - 5 - 7- 2- 4	C-E-G-B-D-F	Cmaj11, Cma11, CM11 C j11 C△11
9/11	1 - 3 - 5 - 2- 4	C-E-G-D-F	C9/11
minor eleventh	1 - 3b - 5 - 7b- 2- 4	C-Eb-G-Bb-D-F	Cm11
thirteenth	1 - 3 - 5 - 6 - 7b- 2	C-E-G-Bb-D-A	C13
minor thirteenth	1 - 3b - 5 - 6 -7b- 2	C-Eb-G-Bb-D-A	Cm13
major thirteenth	1 - 3 - 5 - 6 - 7- 2	C-E-G-B-D-A	Cmaj13, Cma13, CM13 C j13 C△13
6/11	1 - 3 - 5 - 6 - 4	C-E-G-A-F	C6/11

The Root / Bass Note

When we compare two or more notes, our ear usually uses the lower pitched note as a reference and compares the higher notes to it. (This is why if just our lowest string is out of tune, it makes us want to tune the others to it.) **The lowest note of a chord is by far the most important in shaping the flavor and sound of a chord.** Pay attention and keep track of your bass notes. You will notice that most of the chords in this book have 1's or 5's in the bass, though there are a few with unusual bass notes that I liked. Even the musical 3rd can sound odd if it is in the bass. Compare these standard tuning C chords, with 1, 3 or 5 in the bass.

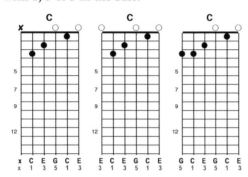

Now listen to the Em chord with the root bass and with the 3rd in the bass. It's almost unusable as a standalone chord:

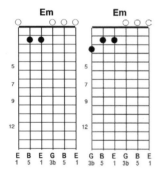

If a 6th, 7th or 9th is in the bass, it may render the chord barely usable. The D major chord with the E bass should be some kind of *Dadd9* chord, but it is really just a "non-chord." We can't compare it to the sound of adding the D note an octave higher on the 4th string, since we can't play that E without removing our D low note on the 4th string. But we can compare the sound of adding a D note to a C chord in 2 octaves. Notice how much better it sounds when added in the treble. Even adding the D in the middle is pretty "muddy."

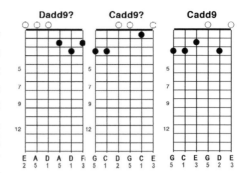

As a general rule, you will get stronger chords if there are roots or 5ths in the bass, with the more "exotic" notes in the treble.

About Dissonance and Pitch

Play an E and an F simultaneously, or any musical interval of a "minor 2nd," which means 2 adjacent keys on the piano. They are quite dissonant. On a guitar play the 6th fret of the B string [F] and the open high E string at the same time. Now separate the notes E-F by an octave and play them again. (This time play fret 2 of the 4th string [E] and the 1st fret of the high E string [F]. The result is much less dissonant. If you play the open bass E [E] and fret 1 of the high E string [F] simultaneously and separate the E from the F by another octave, the interval E-F is not really dissonant anymore.

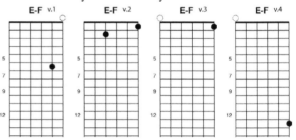

Finally, if you play the bass E string and the 13th fret F on the high E string, this is also the same interval of E-F, except now the two are separated by 3 octaves. It is not dissonant at all.

Sometimes chords and inversions of chords sound fine if they are spread across several octaves, even though the same letter-named notes would not sound as good if they were closer together in overall pitch.

The location of the notes in the chord has a big effect on the sound. If you find a chord you like or don't like in this book, study the structure more carefully.

134

About Numbers like 9ths and 11ths

You've probably noticed that the numerals 1-7 mark the musical function of the chords in this book, yet the chords have names like 9th, 11th and 13th. This is one of those "gray areas" where things are not totally logical, but it is standard practice. To be rigorous, when you add a D note to a C chord, you should call it a 2nd if it is in a lower octave and a 9th if it is higher, and you might wonder why we don't call adding a D note another octave higher a 16th. The answer is that we don't. The language used, like a lot of linguistic things, evolves and changes as it is passed through the people that use it. Musicians tend to use the term "9th chord" when there is a 1-3-5 chord with both a 7th and a 2nd added, but if there is no 7th, and it is just 1-3-5-2 it is called an "*add9*," "*add2*" or "*sus2*." I use the term *add9* in this book, though just as many people call it an add2, and some people use both. Likewise, musicians have adopted the terms 11th and 13th, but you just don't hear talk of 18th or 20th chords, and the distinctions and definitions are often blurred.

There is no legislation or regulation, and not much in the way of organized attempts to standardize things. After decades of independent teachers and publishers inventing notation and terminology, there is quite a lot of diversity in the way music theory is written and discussed. The *Berklee College of Music* in Boston is doing a lot to make the study of contemporary music theory more uniform.

Inversions, Voicings and Doubling

What is also not clear, and something for which there is no terminology, is what happens when there are notes "missing." This happens all the time in guitar, since we have such limitations in fingerings, especially when trying to play extended chords that may have 5 or 6 notes in their "official" form when we only have 4 fingers and 6 strings. What if it is 1-5-7b-2 or 1-3-7b-2? Are they still 9th chords? In this book I say *yes*.

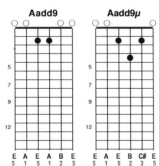

These two *Aadd9* chords are quite different in sound, because one has just 1-2-5 notes and the other has 1-2-3-5. The popular rock band *Steely Dan* made extensive use of these kinds of chords, and called them "*mu*" chords, since

there was no common name for this kind of structure.

Music theory books teach that an "uninverted" or root position C triad has the notes C-E-G, while a 1st inversion C chord has the spelling E-G-C and a 2nd inversion is G-C-E. The term "inversion" is sometimes used to mean the order of notes or voicing, though technically it refers to which is the lowest note in the group.

Look at any groups of chords in this book, and you will see quite a diversity of repeated, scrambled and missing numbers. This is the beauty and mystery of guitar chords, and in this book they are all laid out in front of you.

Those Pesky 4's and 11's

If we add a 4th scale note to a major chord, 1-3-5-4 or 1-3-4-5 we get what most often is called an add11. Adding the 4 in the lower pitches muddies up the sound a lot, unless we remove the 3rd, and just have 1-4-5, which is usually called a "sus," suspended 4th or sus4.

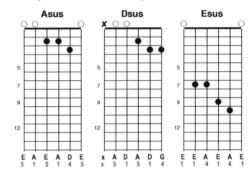

There are all kinds of chords with 4's sprinkled around, and they often have missing notes and irregular structure. The Esus here has no 5th. Is it still an Esus?

The *sus4* is an unstable chord that wants to resolve back to the major. *The Who's* song *Pinball Wizard* is full of them.

It's quite common to have the 3rd replaced with the 4th, and also have a flat 7th. This chord is called the 7th suspended, or 7sus, and there are a lot of them in troubadour's lives.

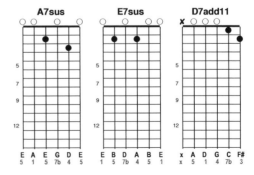

Adding the 4th and the flat 7 without removing the 3rd is often called 7add11 since it is not the same as a 7sus. I use this category in this book.

But what if we add the 4 in a high octave and don't remove

the 3rd? We get a different-sounding kind of *add11* harp-like chord. They are hard to play but sound great. Because of how standard tuning works, these are rare, and there are a lot more of these kinds of "overlapping" voicings that show up when you use open tunings or partial capos:

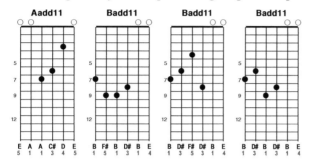

What is normally called an 11th chord in music theory is a chord that has a 1-3-5 foundation, and then it has a 7th, 9th and also an 11th added on. This is a 6-note chord that is much easier on piano than guitar. It's a very different sounding chord than an add11. There are actually a lot of A11 chords. Here are a couple, plus a C11. Notice that they are all missing some notes:

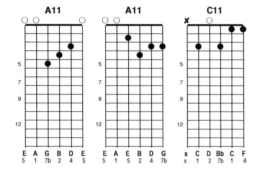

Identifying a Chord

It's one thing to look for ways to play a particular chord on the fingerboard, but it's another task entirely to find a chord, and then wonder what it might be called or how it might be used. Our ears are a big part of this, and we should learn to hear the telltale sound of each type of chords. Many chords are "cut and dried" and everyone agrees what they are called. Others can be ambiguous. No doubt some of you will object to the names I have given to some chords, especially if you are used to using an enharmonic equivalent. The point at which a Em7 chord becomes a G6 is sometimes unclear. If it has a big E bass note on the bottom that will tilt the balance toward calling it an Em7, and if there is a G on the bottom, it will be more of a G6. But what about these D6 and Bm7 chords?

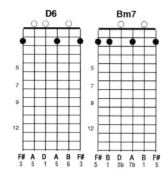

They are much closer in sound, since both have the F# on the bottom. If you lifted that B note on the A string up and down it would not sound that different, but would technically switch the chord from D6 to Bm7. Change a note, add an E on top, and it really becomes a Bm11 with no 9th in it, then add the 9th C# on the B string if you like, or remove the low F# bass note and it's an E7sus.

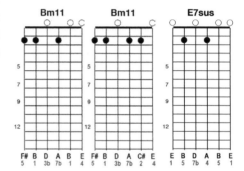

Here is another good example. It's a chord I use to follow 2 frets above an E minor in my instrumental version of Gershwin's *Summertime*:

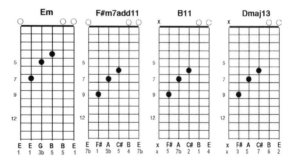

Depending on which note you choose to be the root, you get three totally different names. You tell me what to call it.

Chords Without Good Names

A great example of a chord without a good name is a chord that has been around as long as standard tuning itself. It is the chord you get when you move an E major chord up a half step and still leave the 1-2 and 6 strings open. Or when you slide an A chord up a half step:

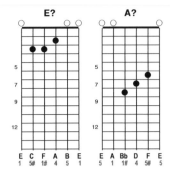

various orders and depending on which bass root note is prominent you can call it a C6/9, Am9, D11, Em11#5, or even something like G6/9/11.

Try to just enjoy the sounds of chords, and use them in your music, and keep an open mind about what to call them. Other people may use different terminology.

It is a very common chord in Spanish and Flamenco music, and there is probably one in the soundtrack of every spaghetti Western movie. It just doesn't fit regular music theory explanations. Instead of E-B-E-G#-B-E (E major chord) you now have E-C-F-A-B-E, which means you sort of still have an E chord, since that is the root, but it has a 4th (A), a "sharp 5" or "flat 6" (C) and what might be called a "sharp 1" or a "flat 2." This chord sounds great when you play first an E chord, then this chord, and then go back to the E chord. It is sometimes called a *"Phrygian suspended"* chord, but the technical explanation of that chord usually just calls it a "sus4 flat9" (b9) which does not mention the other note C. If you play guitar in *Phrygian* mode, you know all about this kind of chord, but other troubadours you run into probably won't know what to call it any more than you do.

Another great example of a chord that has no name and isn't really a useful and functioning chord is the 6 open strings of a standard-tuned guitar: E-A-D-G-B-E. No one uses it in songs or instrumental music, but we all have heard it a lot. Because it has a bass string note of E and a D (7b) and a G (3b) it could be called some kind of extended E minor 7th, with numerical spelling from the E scale as 1-4-7b-3b-5-1. That A note in the bottom end doesn't belong, and the bass end is a poor place to put a 4th. So if you instead thought of it as an A-rooted chord, then the low E string would be a 5th, and the chord would have the spelling: 5-1-4-7b-2-5 which would make it a lousy voicing of an A11th chord, since it has the flat 7th and 2 (9th). But it has no 3rd in this latter situation, which makes it less convincing. Without the E bass note it could be a D-root chord, with added 6/9/11 notes.

There are plenty of other chords you will find that just don't have good names and that don't fit common patterns. The "C-A-G-E-D" chord is one I have been bumping into a lot lately. With those note names in

THE SONG TRAIN (2007) is a landmark resource for beginning guitarists by Harvey Reid & Joyce Andersen. 4-CD boxed set with 80-page color hardback book, contains 56 one & two chord songs. Half the songs are copyrighted, by the likes of Bob Dylan, Hank Williams, Chuck Berry etc, so it offers beginners easy but great songs they can play. Folk, blues, gospel, rock, celtic, country and gospel songs, and an amazing cross-section of American music. **www.songtrain.net**

THE TROUBADOUR GUITAR CHORD BOOK (2013) The best, most complete and readable standard-tuning chord encyclopedia, and an essential new reference tool. A monumental and important new work that may never go back on your shelf. Unlike other large chord books that are tailored for jazz guitarists, the *Troubadour Guitar Chord Book* features over 2900 open and closed-string voicings, optimized and selected for solo acoustic and troubadour-style guitarists.

THE BIG DADGAD CHORD BOOK (2014) The best, most complete and readable chord encyclopedia in DADGAD tuning, with 2500 chords mapped out. Another indispensable reference book for anyone who plays in this popular tuning. Also features full-fingerboard diagrams, with every note and scale degree shown for every chord.

THE BIG BOOK OF BANJO CHORDS (2015) The most complete, detailed and versatile book of chords for standard banjo G tuning. The fingerboard shown like never before, with 5th string notes shown.

THE BIG BOOK OF MANDOCELLO CHORDS (2015) The most complete, detailed and versatile book of chords for standard C-G-A-D tuning. Also includes 11 of the first ideas ever published for partial capos on mandocello.

THE BIG BOOK OF BARITONE UKULELE CHORDS (2015) The most complete, detailed and versatile book of chords for standard D-G-B-E tuning.

BARITONE UKULELE SIMPLIFIED (2015) Explores 9 different new tunings and partial capo ideas that reveal for the first time how to play instant music with great-sounding but simpler chord shapes. This is the first book to introduce partial capos on a ukulele.

SLEIGHT OF HAND (1983) The first book of partial capo guitar arrangements, still in print. 16 solo guitar arrangements using a universal partial capo. Intermediate to advanced level, mostly for fingerstyle guitar, but has 2 flatpicked fiddle tune arrangements (*Sally Goodin'* and *Devil's Dream*) In TAB and standard notation. *Suite: For the Duchess, Für Elise, Scarborough Fair, Minuet in Dm, Flowers of Edinburgh, Simple Gifts, Sally Goodin', Irish Washerwoman, Pavanne, Minuet in Dm, Red-Haired Boy, June Apple, Jesu Joy of Man's Desiring, Devil's Dream, Sally Goodin', Scherzo, Shenandoah, Greensleeves, Sailor's Hornpipe, Fisher's Hornpipe*

CAPO INVENTIONS (2006) 14 intermediate to advanced arrangements from Reid's catalog of guitar recordings. Precisely transcribed for solo guitar, these pieces all use a 3-string *Esus* type partial capo. In TAB and standard notation. *Skye Boat Song, Highwire Hornpipe, Windy Grave, Hard Times, The Unknown Soldier, Suite: For the Duchess, The Arkansas Traveler, The Minstrel Boy, Red in the Sky, Prelude to the Minstrel's Dream, Norway Suite: Parts 1 &2, Star Island Jig, Macallan's Jig.*

THE LIBERTY "FLIP" CAPO IDEA BOOKS (2014-15) Two volumes, totaling almost 400 pages, with over 113 ideas of partial capo configurations that can be done with a pair of *Model 43* and *Model 65 Liberty* partial capos. These were developed by Harvey Reid, and are the new generation of sleek and versatile partial capos that clamp 6, 5, 4 or 3 strings on most guitars, banjos, ukes and mandolins. Volume I shows 72 ideas, mostly in standard tuning, and with a taste of combining capos with altered tunings. Volume 2 combines capos with altered tunings.

SECRETS OF THE 3-STRING PARTIAL CAPO (2010) 24 mind-bending ways to use the popular 3-string *Esus* (*E-suspended*) type partial capo. *This book may no longer be available after the arrival of the Liberty Capos.* 18 of these ideas are now in the *Liberty Capo IDEA BOOK* , and the other 6 appear in the *Liberty "FLIP" Capo IDEA BOOK Vol.2.*

MORE SECRETS OF THE 3-STRING PARTIAL CAPO (2013) 27 more ways to use 3-string *Esus* (*E-suspended*) type partial capos. **12 of these ideas are now in the *Liberty Capo IDEA BOOK* , and the others are in the *Liberty Capo IDEA BOOK Vol.2.***

SECRETS OF THE 4 & 5-STRING PARTIAL CAPOS (2011) Another treasure trove of ideas, for the *Planet Waves*, *Shubb*, or *Kyser* shortened 4 or 5-string capos. (Also valuable for *Third Hand, Liberty "Flip"* or *Spider* universal capos.) Most people who have one of these capos know a few ways to use them. Here are an amazing 47 ideas that use a 4 or 5-string capo to generate new music. Over 1600 chords. *This book may no longer be available after the arrival of the Liberty Capos.* **30 of these 47 ideas are now in the *Liberty Capo IDEA BOOK* , and the other 17 appear in the *Liberty Capo IDEA BOOK Vol.2.***

SECRETS OF THE 1 & 2-STRING PARTIAL CAPOS (2012) How to use the unique *Woodie's G-Band* 1 and 2-string partial capos. 33 clever ways to use these capos in a number of tunings and in combination with other partial capos, with over 1100 chords. 98 pages are packed with photos, ideas and capo knowledge that is only available here. Even the makers of the capos don't know about these ideas.

SECRETS OF PARTIAL CAPOS IN DADGAD TUNING (2012) Most people think of partial capos as a substitute for open tunings, and don't realize that they can be combined. Harvey Reid shows you over 25 ingenious ways to use partial capos to expand the musical possibilities of DADGAD tuning (4 of them use the similar CGDGAD tuning.) Get new chords, fingerings, voicings, resonances and unlock a new, mysterious world of new music hiding in your fingerboard. **17 of these ideas are now in the *Liberty Capo IDEA BOOK Vol.2.***

SECRETS OF UNIVERSAL PARTIAL CAPOS (2012) 45 ways to get new music from your guitar that can only be done with universal partial capos. This hidden world of music in your fingerboard includes a number of tunings and combinations with other partial capos. Over 1500 chords. Packed with photos, clear explanations and capo strategy will save you years of searching. **Because the *Model 43 Liberty* capo clamps 4 middle strings, 13 of these ideas are now duplicated in the *Liberty Capo IDEA BOOKS, Vol. 1-2.***

SECRETS OF PARTIAL CAPOS IN DROP D TUNING (2014) The most common tuning is *Drop D*: D A D G B E, and like any tuning, it can be combined with partial capos to add another dimension to the guitar. This book presents 24 ways to use one or more partial capos of all types to generate more new music. **9 of these ideas are now in the *Liberty Capo IDEA BOOK*, and 7 more appear in *Vol.2.*** The others use a universal or *G-Band* capo.

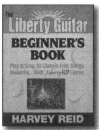

THE LIBERTY GUITAR BEGINNER'S BOOK (2015) Play 30 classic folk songs instantly with super-simple, great-sounding chords. For children or adults, this book carefully explains how to use *Liberty Tuning* to play chords and sing songs in 6 different major and minor keys. You need a guitar, a full capo, and a *Liberty FLIP Model 43* capo.

THE LIBERTY TUNING CHORD BOOK (2013) In his partial capo research, Harvey Reid discovered a simple new guitar tuning that introduces a remarkable geometrical symmetry and simplicity to the guitar fingerboard that no one ever dreamed existed. Here is a thorough examination of what this amazing tuning can do, with over 1200 chords, sorted, mapped out and organized to help you find your way in *Liberty Tuning*. Lots of tips, advice & clear explanations. For guitar teachers, beginners and anyone who already plays guitar and wants to learn about this important discovery.

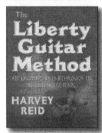

THE LIBERTY GUITAR METHOD (2013) Total beginners can play music like never before. It's easy to do and sounds great. Learn to use *Liberty Tuning* to play great-sounding, simple 2-finger chords to songs by Bob Dylan, Hank Williams, John Prine, Johnny Cash, Chuck Berry, The Beatles, Adele, and more. You won't believe it 'til you try it. *Hush Little Baby, This Land is Your Land, Your Cheating Heart, A Hard Rain's A Gonna Fall, Amazing Grace, The Cuckoo, Folsom Prison Blues, Angel From Montgomery, Maybellene, Let It Be, Imagine, Someone Like You, The Wedding Song, House of the Rising Sun*

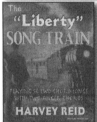

THE LIBERTY SONG TRAIN (2013) Learn how to use *Liberty Tuning* to play all 56 two-chord songs in the epic *Song Train* collection with just 2-finger chords, in the same keys as they were done on the *Song Train* recordings. Beginning guitar has never been easier. Careful explanations, with lots of helpful tips, strategy and advice. If you have the *Song Train* 4-CD collection, you need this companion book.

LIBERTY GUITAR FOR KIDS (2013) It's a huge breakthrough in children's guitar. Children as young as 4 can learn to strum simple 2-finger *Liberty Tuning* chords and play guitar like never before. Classic traditional plus modern children's songs arranged in keys young voices can sing in. No need to wait until the children grow bigger or waste your money on crummy small children's guitars. Learn how even small children can instantly start strumming songs on adult guitars. It's really amazing. *London Bridge, Row Row Row Your Boat, Farmer in the Dell, Hush Little Baby, This Land is Your Land, Oh Susannah, Standing in the Need of Prayer, Hey Lolly Lolly, Comin' Round the Mountain* and more.

THE 2-FINGER GUITAR GUIDE (2013) A careful study of simplified guitar chords, this book takes you through each of the common tunings and partial capo configurations that can be used to play simplified guitar chords. Learn the advantages and disadvantages of each of 28 different guitar environments, including the amazing *Liberty Tuning* and related hybrid tunings. If you have a shortage of fingers on the fretting hand, or if you work with hand injuries, special music education or music therapy, this is the definitive guide to showing what can be done musically with just 2-finger chords.

www.woodpecker.com

ABOUT THE AUTHOR

Harvey Reid has been a full-time acoustic guitar player since 1974, and has performed over 6000 concerts throughout the US and in Europe. He won the 1981 *National Fingerpicking Guitar Competition* and the 1982 *International Autoharp* contest, and has released 32 highly-acclaimed recordings of original, traditional and contemporary acoustic music.

He is best known for his solo fingerstyle guitar work, but he is also a solid flatpicker (he won Bill Monroe's *Beanblossom* bluegrass guitar contest in 1976), a versatile singer, lyricist, prolific composer, arranger and songwriter. He also plays mandolin and bouzouki. Reid recorded the first album ever of 6 & 12-string banjo music, and his CD *Solo Guitar Sketchbook* made GUITAR PLAYER MAGAZINE's Top 20 essential acoustic guitar CD's list. His CD *Steel Drivin' Man* was chosen by ACOUSTIC GUITAR MAGAZINE as one of **Top 10 Folk CD's** of all time, along with Woody Guthrie, Ry Cooder and other hallowed names. His music was included in the blockbuster BBC TV show *A Musical Tour of Scotland*, and Reid was featured in the Rhino Records **Acoustic Music of the 90's** collection, along with a "who's who" line-up of other artists including Richard Thompson, Jerry Garcia & Leo Kottke.

In 1980 Reid published *A New Frontier in Guitar*, the first book about the partial capo, and in 1984 he wrote *Modern Folk Guitar*, the first college textbook for folk guitar. Quite possibly the first modern person to publish and record with the partial capo, he is almost certainly the most prolific arranger and composer of partial capo guitar music, and is responsible for most of what is known about the device. He lives in southern Maine with his family.

Printed in Great Britain
by Amazon

57035597R00084